TIMELY MESSAGES
For Times Like These

Books by J. Guy Cothran
THE CHRISTIAN FAMILY
THE VICTORIOUS CHRISTIAN LIFE
THE CHRISTIAN'S HOME IN GLORY

An Acknowledgement

I am indebted to Mrs. Cothran for the work she has done in reading and checking the Manuscript for any errors or incorrect statements. I am also indebted to Mrs. Edward (Shirley) Timmerman who was of great help in typing the Manuscript.

TIMELY MESSAGES

For Times Like These

By J. Guy Cothran

DROKE HOUSE, *Publishers*

ANDERSON, SOUTH CAROLINA

Distributed By

GROSSET & DUNLAP

51 Madison Avenue, New York, N. Y.

TIMELY MESSAGES
Copyright © 1970 by J. Guy Cothran

All Rights Reserved

First Edition

Standard Book Number: 8375-6752-1
Library of Congress Catalog Card Number: 72-123356

Manufactured In The United States of America

Dedication

This book is affectionately dedicated to all preachers who have served to inspire, teach, and encourage me in my ministry to peoples with whom I have worked through the years.

It is sent forth with a desire that the lives of those who read it will be blessed and that they in turn will bless the lives of others in their ministry of love.

CONTENTS

INTRODUCTION

Here is another work from the pen and experience of J. Guy Cothran. We are indebted to him for *The Victorious Christian Life, The Christian Family,* and *The Christian's Home in Glory.* This author, who has served as pastor, and teacher for many years, uses the sermon as an effective instrument of teaching. These books will enrich the life of any pastor or layman who feels the need for instruction in Christian faith.

Mr. Cothran was born in Greenville County, S. C. and received his Bachelor of Arts degree from Furman University and the Master of Theology degree from Southern Baptist Theological Seminary in 1925.

This man has had a long and fruitful ministry in Kentucky, Florida, Arkansas and South Carolina. When he returned to his native state, he served as pastor of the Beaverdam Baptist Church in Anderson County and taught Bible at Anderson College. His service to the Baptist denomination has been faithful and varied. All of his experience has been enriched by extensive travel in the Near East, South America, Europe, and Africa.

It has been my privilege to know J. Guy Cothran for a number of years, the last eight of which I have served as his pastor.

In this book are sermons for "special days". Mr. Cothran

uses to advantage the interest of the moment to present the eternal verities of God. The devotional sermons and other messages come out of his experience in the pulpit and will meet a need for all Christian people.

These messages will stimulate thought, or afford suggestions that may aid the teacher in preparation for the class, or stimulate the preacher in preparation for a particular message. For any of God's children, these messages should provide comfort and encouragement as they face the opportunities and responsibilities of the Christian life.

Marion H. Hare, Pastor
Augusta Road Baptist Church
Greenville, South Carolina

PREFACE

We are living in a day when there are many things that are troubling people. We need to know the things that will not pass away as history and geography are changing and will continue to change.

Everything is not going to fall in about us. It may seem that way during times of war, revolution, and disaster. However, God is still keeping an eye on the affairs of mankind. Men are not going to out-think and out-wit God. He still keeps His eye on the time when history will be consumated.

The messages in this book deal with great and eternal verities that will not perish with the changes that come. We need to know where we are going. We need to be anchored in God. We need to listen to God as He speaks in His Word to our hearts and minds in the NOW. There are messages that are timeless. They were good in the long ago. They are good for the generation of which we are a part. They will be good for the generations which are yet to be born.

God is timeless. God's truth goes marching on. God's redemptive plan for the ages is timeless. Jesus is the same in all times.

J. Guy Cothran

CHAPTER ONE

LOOKING INTO THE NEW YEAR
A New Year's Message

It is good for us to stop and think as we come to the beginning of a New Year. It is good for us to take stock. People get all fouled up and entangled with things that are destructive and devitalizing. Some very familiar words have been written by an unknown author. They are:

"And I said to the man who stood at the gate of the year:

Give me a light that I may tread softly into the unknown!

And he replied: Go out into the darkness and put thine hand into the hand of God.

That shall be to thee better than light and safer than a known way."

In Revelation 21:5 we find a most significant statement. God says, "Behold I make all things new." Paul speaks of how old things (that is, those things of a sinful nature) have passed away and "all things are become new". 2 Corinthians 5:17. There are many things spoken of as being new. We have a new life in Christ. John speaks of having a new name written on a white stone. The psalmist speaks of a new song. Peter speaks of looking "for new heavens and a new earth, wherein dwelleth righteousness." 2 Peter 3:13. So as we face the new year let us think of the things old and new that have been provided for us. Let us resolve to give ourselves to things that make for living the new life as it will be honoring to God and helpful to our fellowman. The beginning of the New Year is indeed a time of beginning again.

"I wish there were some wonderful place,
Called the land of beginning again,
Where all our mistakes and all our heartaches,
And all our selfish grief could be dropped,
Like a shabby old coat at the door,
And never put on again."

Author Unknown

IT IS GOOD FOR US TO LOOK BACK

There are many good things to think about as we look back. Of course, there have been failures and mistakes made during the past year. These can serve as stumbling stones or as stepping stones. The Apostle Paul could look back with profit. We are not to live in the past. However, there are some things that are most helpful to consider as we look back. We can think of the good that we have done and the blessings that have come to us along the journey. It is good for us to forget the injuries and the hurts of the past and do as Paul — "reaching forth unto those things which are before, I press toward the mark for the prize of the high calling of God in Christ Jesus." Phil. 3:13-14. It is my joy and delight to claim friendship with some people who have lived helpfully and effectively for almost one hundred years. I have two friends who are husband and wife. They have been married for more than sixty-five years. He has been a minister of the Gospel for more than sixty years. We still write fairly regularly. In one of the recent letters was this interesting statement: "Here we sit, two old persons facing the evening tide of life with no children, no grandchildren, no nothing, but a lot of pleasant memories." So it is with all of us who live and live usefully — we too can have pleasant memories that will make the evening tide of life worth while.

LOOK AT YOUR LIFE IN THE
LIGHT OF GOD'S MIRROR

James 1:22-25 pictures a man looking into a mirror of God's word and beholding himself. Then he goes away to do something about what has been revealed to him in the light of the Word of God. The scripture says "this man shall be blessed in his deeds". Some people see in the mirror what they are and seek to do something that will make them better and really "a doer of the word". God's Word will show us what we are in our sinful state, and will also show us what we ought to be, and what we can be by His grace. We are to set our affections on things above. We are to be concerned about laying up treasure in Heaven. Too many people are earth-bound. It would be most helpful if we would pray as the Psalmist, "Search me, O God, and know my heart: try me and know my thoughts: and see if there be any wicked way in me, and lead me in the way everlasting." Psalm 139:23-24. Again we read, "I said I will take heed to my ways, that I sin not with my tongue: I will keep my mouth with a bridle, while the wicked is before me." Psalm 39:1.

There are so many beautiful things to behold in nature. There are the many sunsets that we look upon that speak of the Great Artist. Many fail to see and smell the fragrance of the lovely flowers that bloom along our pathway. There is the singing of the birds which to some is so much noise. So many times we fail to see the good that others do and the good that is within them. If we would look for the good we would see it. There are people who take the worm's eye view of life. Bunyan's muck raker saw mud. "Two men looked through prison bars. The one saw mud, the other saw stars."

AS WE FACE THE NEW YEAR LET US LOOK TO GOD

There is salvation in a look. "Look unto me, and be ye saved, all the ends of the earth: for I am God, and there is none else." Isaiah 45:22. When the people in the wilderness were bitten by poisonous snakes Moses made a brazen serpent. The people were to look in faith to the up-lifted serpent and by so doing would be healed. Of course, it was not the serpent that healed, but God. Jesus himself said, "And as Moses lifted up the serpent in the wilderness, even so must the Son of man be lifted up; that whosoever believeth on him should not perish, but have everlasting life." John 3:14-15. Following this is that great verse, "For God so loved the world, that he gave his only begotten son, that whosoever believeth in him should not perish, but have everlasting life." Yes, if a sinner is to have life it will come to him as he looks in faith believing that God is willing and able to save him even unto the uttermost. How true it is, "Look to Jesus now and live. Tis recorded in His Word, hallelujah, it is only that you look and live." Jesus said, "And I, if I be lifted up from the earth, will draw all men unto me." One of the great hymns has in it these wonderful words:

"My faith looks up to thee,
Thou Lamb of Calvary, Savior Divine;
Now hear me while I pray,
Take all my guilt away,
O let me from this day be wholly thine!"

We should look to God for strength. This is needed for each step of the way. The psalmist could truly say, "God is my refuge and strength, a very present help in trouble . . . ." Psalm 46:1. He could also say, "I will lift up mine eyes unto the hills, from whence cometh my help. My help cometh from the Lord, who made heaven and earth." Psalm 121:1-2.

16

Again we find in Psalm 27:1 these helpful words, "The Lord is my light and my salvation; whom shall I fear? The Lord is the strength of my life; of whom shall I be afraid?"

We should look to God for wisdom and guidance. "If any of you lack wisdom, let him ask of God, that giveth to all men liberally and upbraideth not; and it shall be given him." James 1:5. God was manifest in the pillar of cloud by day and the pillar of fire by night. This gave the children of Israel and Moses assurance that God would go before them and that he would be behind them to deliver them. Someone said, "I had rather walk in the dark with God than to walk in the light alone."

A wise statement is made in Proverbs 3:5-6: "Trust in the Lord with all thine heart; and lean not unto thine own understanding. In all thy ways acknowledge him, and he shall direct thy paths." No person can safely tread the way of this New Year without God. Only God knows what each day of the year will bring to us. We should pray daily the words in an old hymn — "Guide me, O thou great Jehovah, pilgrim through this barren land." This walk down the corridor of the new year will be a walk of faith. We are to walk by faith and not by sight. The man of faith can say what a missionary long ago said as he faced his task: "Hats off to the past, coats off to the future." We are to move forward. When the people came in their journey to the Red Sea and had been standing still, God said to Moses, "Speak to the Children of Israel that they go forward." This they did. They could not see how, with mountains on either side, the sea before them, and the Egyptian army close behind, but God opened the way as they moved forward.

At a time when the battle was going hard, a little drummer boy was told to beat a retreat. He replied, "Sir, I have never learned to beat a retreat." God's people are to move forward under the guidance and leadership of God

17

toward the city of God.

AS WE LOOK TOWARD THE NEW YEAR
LET US LOOK AT A LOST AND NEEDY WORLD

Jesus said, "Lift up your eyes, and look on the fields; for they are white already to harvest." John 4:35. Jesus was always concerned with lost people. He showed His interest, compassion, and concern by doing something for the lost. He invited them to come to Him for help. He saved all who came trustingly and believingly to Him. When He saved those who became His apostles and disciples He sent them out, commanded and commissioned to search for and to bring the lost to Him for salvation from their sins. He truly said, "For the Son of man is come to seek and to save that which was lost . . ." Matthew 1:21 says "and thou shalt call his name JESUS: for he shall save his people from their sins." We are to pray for more laborers to gather in the harvest. Every saved person is commissioned to go with the message of good news to all the people of the earth. We are to begin where we are, telling the good news to those of our own household. We are to tell the lost where we work that we have a Savior who can and will save. This was His purpose in coming from heaven to earth.

DURING THE NEW YEAR LET US
RUN THE RACE AS VICTORS

In Hebrews 12:1-2 the writer gives us a great text for a new year's message. Read it and ponder it for the practical help and inspiration it will bring to your heart. "Wherefore seeing we also are compassed about with so great a cloud of witnesses, let us lay aside every weight, and the sin which doth so easily beset us, and let us run with patience the race that is set before us.

Looking unto Jesus the author and finisher of our faith;

who for the joy that was set before him, endured the cross, despising the shame, and is set down at the right hand of the throne of God." This text is the conclusion of what goes before in the Faith chapter. Witnesses on earth and in heaven seem to be looking upon the Christian runner. Surely all who are God's saints pray for and desire victory for every other Christian. The Lord is also looking upon us and counting upon us. If we run the race and come to the end of the journey as victors there are some things we must do. We must lay aside sin. We must lay aside any weight that would hinder. Runners go through rigid exercise. One must be willing to pay the price if one is to win. It takes patience and persistence to run the Christian race. If he runs in the Olympics he must be governed by certain rules. He does not make the rules. So must every Christian run according to Christian principles. One of the big things for a runner in an Olympic event is to be physically fit. In the Christian race one who has a weak body or who is physically handicapped can run and can be a winner.

In this race the runner must keep his eyes upon Jesus. "Looking unto Jesus the author and the finisher of our faith . . . ." The secret of a tight rope walker is that he keeps his eyes upon where he is going. Driving a car safely means that the driver must keep his eyes on the road. We are to keep our minds on our objective and aim in life. Every Christian should have a worthy goal. To attain the desired goal you must bend every energy in that direction. Jesus thought of that which would be accomplished in his death on the cross. He also had in mind the joy that would be his beyond the suffering of the cross. How true are the words of a chorus we sing — "Turn your eyes upon Jesus. Look full in his wonderful face and the things of earth will grow strangely dim in the light of his glory and grace." When the disciples came down from a glorious experience on the Mount of

Transfiguration "They saw no man but Jesus only".

Regardless of how many days you will have the privilege of walking, living, and serving during this New Year you can be a victor. As a Christian living according to the rules you can overcome every day. "For we are more than conquerors through him that loved us" assures us of victory. "To him that overcometh will I grant to sit with me in my throne, even as I also overcame, and am set down with my father in his throne" (Revelation 3:21) assures us of reward.

CONCLUSION

Every Christian has a race to run. He has a warfare to fight. He has a faith to live by and to keep. Paul, as he came near the close of his life's work felt that there was something laid up in store for him and for all who were faithful. That is why he could say, "Henceforth there is laid up for me a crown of righteousness, which the Lord, the righteous judge, shall give me at that day: and not to me only, but to all them also that love His appearing." 2 Timothy 4:8. Those of us who walk by faith down through this New Year can sing with assurance those wonderful words penned by the hymn writer.

> To him that overcometh, God giveth a crown,
> Through faith we shall conquer, though often cast down;
> He who is our Savior, our strength will renew;
> Look ever to Jesus He'll carry you through.

Chorus:
> Ask the Savior to help you,
> Comfort, strengthen and keep you,
> He is willing to aid you,
> He will carry you through.

CHAPTER TWO

THE RESURRECTION STORY
An Easter Message
1 Cor. 15, Acts 2:22-34
Matt. 28:1-15

One of the best established facts of the Bible is the fact that Jesus arose from the grave. For the person with an open and an inquiring mind there is proof in the Holy Scriptures that the grave was found empty on the third day. *Many* testified to this fact. Reliable witnesses saw the Risen Lord. Jesus appeared to *many* on the Resurrection Day and during the days that followed.

In the sermon that Peter preached at Pentecost he emphasized the fact that this Jesus who had been crucified had come forth a victor over death and the grave. Peter could stand up and speak with boldness about the resurrection. He said, "This Jesus hath God raised up, whereof we are all witnesses . . . . Therefore let all the house of Israel know assuredly, that God hath made that same Jesus, whom ye have crucified, both Lord and Christ." Acts 2:32, 36.

Jesus talked much about his coming death, burial, and resurrection. The whole of his teachings rests upon the Doctrine of the Resurrection. It is indeed the keystone in the arch of Christianity. Take this out of the Christian religion

21

and the whole structure will collapse. The hope of the resurrection enables us to look beyond the grave.

THERE CANNOT BE ANY GOSPEL
WITHOUT THE RESURRECTION

The Scripture plainly states: "He is not here: for he is risen, as he said, Come, see the place where the Lord lay." Matthew 28:6. Again we hear the Apostle say, "If in this life only we have hope in Christ, we are of all men most miserable." 1 Corinthians 15:19. The Gospel of the resurrection is indeed good news. "Moreover, brethren, I declare unto you the Gospel which I preached unto you, which also ye have received, and wherein ye stand . . . ." 1 Corinthians 15:1. The early disciples needed to know the reality of this Gospel. They had become discouraged and felt that the cause to which they had given themselves was a lost cause. The resurrection of Jesus gave them assurance and encouragement and hope for the future. Never again did the disciples question the claims of Jesus. When the disciples saw the risen Lord doubts were dispelled, their faith was confirmed, and they were encouraged for their task. "With great power gave the apostles witness of the resurrection of the Lord Jesus: and great grace was upon them all." Acts 4:33. Paul declares, "For if any man preach any other Gospel unto you . . . let him be acursed." Galatians 1:9.

In the bright light of the resurrection story no person need be ashamed of the Gospel. We should rejoice in the privilege and the responsibility of declaring it to all the people of the world. Had Paul not been assured of the resurrection story he could not have said, "I am not ashamed of the Gospel of Christ: for it is the power of God unto salvation unto every one that believeth; to the Jew first, and also to the Greek." Romans 1:16.

SUPPOSE THERE IS NO RESURRECTION

Of course, this is the kind of argument which is contrary to fact. Paul raises the question to show how vain and meaningless our faith would be if there were no resurrection. Christ would still be in the grave were there no resurrection. If there were no resurrection then our preaching would be vain, empty, and useless. We would be found to be false witnesses if Christ did not arise from the dead. We would still be in our sins if the grave still contained Him. Those who die would go out like a light. Some people believe and teach that death is the end. If there is no resurrection then we would find that our faith is in vain.

FUNDAMENTALS IN THE STORY OF THE RESURRECTION

We could go to scientists and ask them what they think of the resurrection. We would find that some believe in it while others doubt it. We could ask the greatest philosophers what they think, and we would find that some accept this doctrine while others question the reality of it. Wherein does our authority rest in this profound matter? It is in the Bible. As we read the scriptures we find that one called Jesus did live. One day on a hill outside a city wall this One was crucified. We discover that He was buried in the grave of Joseph of Arimathea. This same Jesus who lived, died, and was buried on the third day came forth out of the grave in which he was buried. After ministering and moving among His disciples Jesus ascended on high. We are told by men of integrity that Jesus is coming again. This same Jesus will come again as he went away into heaven. If there were no resurrection of the dead then there would be no need for Jesus to come back. In fact there would be no Jesus to come back if there is no truth in the doctrine of the resurrection.

EVIDENCES OF THE RESURRECTION

In examining any situation or case in point one should look at authentic facts that are involved. Jesus himself tells us that the resurrection is a fact. "For as Jonah was three days and nights in the whale's belly: so shall the son of man be three days and three nights in the heart of the earth." Matthew 12:40.

We find that the son of man must be crucified, buried, and rise again. Jesus stated, "I lay down my life of myself . . . no man taketh it from me . . . ." Jesus did not die because He could not help it. He did not die as a martyr. He willingly and voluntarily laid down His life for sinners. Some of those who saw the empty grave tried to frame some report as to what had happened to the body of Jesus. Some told that his disciples stole away his body. The angel said. "He is not here: for he is risen, as he said. Come, see the place where the Lord lay." Matthew 28:6. Multitudes of people have seen the empty tomb. I, myself, walked in and out of that empty tomb.

THE RECORD SPEAKS

On the day that Jesus came out of the tomb He was seen by many people. Mary saw him in the Garden. Other women saw him also. Peter who had warmed at the enemy's fire and who determined to go fishing so as to ease his disappointment saw him also. Two men were walking along the road to Emmaus, and saw him and talked with him. On a Sunday night in an upper room with Judas and Thomas absent the ten disciples were there when Jesus appeared.

On the second Lord's day following the resurrection of Jesus He was in the upper room with the disciples again. Thomas was present in this meeting. As he saw the scars in the hands, feet, and side of Jesus he could cry out, "My Lord and my God." Early one morning Jesus was down by the sea side. It was here that He ate with seven of his disciples. It was here that Jesus questioned Peter as to whether he loved him or not. As Peter declared and affirmed his love, Jesus commanded him to feed, tend, and take care of his sheep. James saw the risen Lord on at least one occasion. Just before Jesus went back to heaven about 500 people watched him as He went away. Paul asserts that he as though he had been born out of due time saw the risen Lord.

Many people saw Jesus with their own eyes. We do not have that privilege. However, some day we shall see him. When we see him we shall be like him for we shall see him as he is. We sing about Jesus living and reigning within our hearts. "You ask me how I know He lives . . . He lives within my heart." A woman dying from TB was asked if she were afraid to die. She pointed to a motto on the wall of her room. It read, "The gift of God is eternal life".

HOPE NOW AND BEYOND

Paul asked, "If in this life only we have hope in Christ, we are of all men most miserable." 1 Corinthians 15:19. People with and people without faith in the resurrection should read 1 Corinthians 15 over and over again. This is the greatest passage in all the Bible on the ressurrection and that which lies beyond the grave. Look at the hope of one man over against the hopelessness of another! When the brother of Bob Ingersol died Ingersol had the last words to say at the funeral. Bob Ingersol was a so-called infidel, but a very brilliant man. He said, "Life is a narrow vale between the cold and barren peaks of two eternities. We strive in vain to look beyond the heights. We cry aloud and the only answer is the echo of the wailing cry."

Dwight L. Moody stood before the casket in which his brother was cold in death. The man of faith and hope quoted from 1 Corinthians 15. "O death, where is thy sting? O grave, where is thy victory? The sting of death is sin; and the strength of sin is the law. But thanks be unto God, who giveth us the victory through our Lord Jesus Christ."

THERE IS POWER IN THE GOSPEL
OF THE RESURRECTION

At this season of the year tons and tons of life giving sap is drawn up into trees. There is not any noise to be heard as this work of nature is in operation. All about us we see evidences of power at work within the realm of nature. To preach and to teach that there is no such thing as the resurrection of the dead cuts out the very hope and heart of the Gospel. The New Testament speaks of the death, burial, and resurrection of Christ. It also speaks of the death of the sinner to sin, his burial of the old life, and a coming forth of a new creature to walk in newness of life with Christ. The ordinance of the Lord's Supper tells of the death of Jesus, and points to the return of our Lord to earth. This ordinance is to be observed until Christ comes back again to claim His own. The sinner is quickened according to Ephesians 2:1. Since we are risen with Christ we are to seek those things that are above where Christ is at the right hand of God (Colossians 3:1-4). It is significant that at the grave of Lazarus while Mary and Martha were grieving that Jesus would have said what he did. The two sisters believed in a resurrection. Jesus said, "Thy brother shall rise again." It was Martha who said, "I know that he shall rise again in the resurrection at the last day." It was then that Jesus declared, "I am the resurrection and the life: he that believeth in me, though he were dead, yet shall he live: and whosoever liveth and believeth in me shall never die. Believest thou this?" John 11:21-26.

John the beloved disciple of Jesus points with hope to that which lies beyond this life. He said, "Beloved, now are we the sons of God, and it doth not yet appear what we shall be: but we know that when he shall appear, we shall be like him; for we shall see him as he is. And every man that hath this hope in him purifieth himself, even as he is pure." 1 John 3:2-3. In the book of Revelation 1:18 we find these assuring words: "I am he that liveth, and was dead; and behold, I am alive for evermore." Jesus himself stated: "Because I live ye shall live also."

If we turn away from the story of the resurrection where can we turn for comfort and help when death comes and takes away from us those that we hold dear? Jesus came to make salvation available to man. He died, was buried, and arose from the dead to give us hope for that experience that will come to one and to all. We do not have to walk through the valley alone. We do not have to cross Jordan alone. He has traveled this way. He knows the way. He is the way, the truth, and the life.

It was my privilege to hear Dr. Wallace Bassett preach several times. He lived to a ripe old age. He was pastor of the Cliff Temple Baptist Church, Dallas, Texas, for more than fifty years.

One night he baptized a little girl. Her mother, sister, and many others looked on. The smaller child was a little frightened about her sister being put under the water. When the big, strong preacher brought her up out of the watery grave the little sister turned to her mother and said, "Mother, I knew Dr. Bassett would not leave her under." Some time following this Mrs. Bassett died and was buried in the family cemetery. The words of the little girl came to the preacher. As he looked beyond the grave to the bright and glad tomorrow the preacher could say, "I knew that Jesus would not leave her under."

So to those of us who give up our loved ones we can rest assured that Jesus will not leave them in the grave. We have all, no doubt, had a feeling of sadness when we would think of a loved one lying in the cold, cold ground with the rain, and snows falling upon the grave. However, we can say with the angel, "He is not here, for he has risen as he said." As we pay respect to our deceased loved ones we can know that they are at peace with God if they have died in the Lord. "Blessed are the dead who die in the Lord, from henceforth: yea, saith the Spirit, that they may rest from their labors; and their works do follow them." Revelation 14:13.

Why do we sing about the resurrection in the spring of the year: Do we sing with a bright and burning hope within that because Jesus lived we shall live also? Because he came forth out of the grave a victor, we, too, shall be raised? During the post-resurrection days Jesus dispelled the doubt that was in the minds of many. Their faith was rekindled. These once baffled and broken disciples went forth with a fresh and a renewed devotion to the risen Christ. They could indeed say with all assurance, We have seen the Lord, for he is risen as he said.

THE GOSPEL OF THE RESURRECTION
GIVES US HOPE FOR THE BEYOND
"Low in the grave He lay — Jesus my Saviour!
Waiting the coming day — Jesus my Lord!
Vainly they watch His bed — Jesus my Savior!
Vainly they seal the dead — Jesus my Lord!
Death cannot keep his prey — Jesus my Savior!
He tore the bars away — Jesus my Lord!
Chorus:
Up from the grave He arose,
With a mighty triumph o'er his foes;
He arose a victor from the dark domain,
And He lives forever with His saints to reign.
He arose! He arose!

28

Hallelujah! Christ arose!

By Robert Lowry

We know that there is a life beyond the grave. Death does not end all. We are bound for an eternity. That eternity will be in Heaven or in Hell. If we do not have hope beyond the grave then as Paul reminds us in 1 Corinthians 15 we are most miserable. Our preaching is vain and empty if there is no life beyond. The inspired writer could say, "For we know that if our earthly house of this tabernacle were dissolved, we have a building of God, an house not made with hands, eternal in the heavens." 2 Corinthians 5:1. That which is for the child of God beyond this vail is far more wonderful than we can imagine. Paul says, "Eye hath not seen, nor ear heard, neither have entered into the heart of man, the things which God hath prepared for them that love him." 1 Corinthians 2:9.

CHAPTER THREE

JESUS AND WOMANHOOD
Mother's Day
Luke 1:46-56

"And Mary said, My soul doth magnify the Lord, and my spirit hath rejoiced in God my Savior. For he hath regarded the low estate of his handmaiden: for, behold from henceforth all generations shall call me blessed." Luke 1:46-48.

In these verses we find what is called the Magnificat. It is indeed the song of the soul of Mary in which she expresses the joy of her deepest being to God for that which He is about to do for "his handmaiden". It is good for us to consider the low-estate of women before Jesus came to be born of a woman. In pagan and heathen lands woman was considered to be the slave of man. She was not to be thought of as co-equal of man. It has been said, "Back of every great man is a good woman". Emerson said, "Men are what their mothers make them." Carlyle said, "No able man ever had a fool for a mother." Roebuck said, "Heaven is at the feet of mothers." Someone else said, "The hand that rocks the cradle rules the world." Abe Lincoln said, "All that I am or hope to be, I owe to my angel mother." In writing to young Timothy, Paul gave a wise word of counsel in 1 Timothy

5:14 — "I will therefore that the younger women marry, bear children, guide the house, give none occasion to the adversary to speak reproachfully." It has been said by one long ago:

The greatest word is God,
The deepest word is soul,
The longest word is eternity,
The swiftest word is time,
The nearest word is now,
The darkest word is sin,
The meanest word is hypocrisy,
The broadest word is truth,
The strongest word is right,
The tenderest word is love,
The sweetest word is home,
The dearest word is mother.

Surely to have a Christian mother is one of life's greatest blessings bestowed upon any child. Any child born into the world to be trained, nurtured, and loved by a Christ honoring mother is most fortunate.

CONSIDER THE LOW ESTATE OF WOMAN
WHEN JESUS CAME INTO THE WORLD

Woman in the pagan and heathen world was at a low level. Women were no more than chattel in most of the known world. Polygamy was almost universal. Morals were very low. There was no high standard of marriage. Man could use woman as a servant, slave, or a plaything or one to be put away if he so desired. According to Roman law women had no legal rights. One of the wise philosophers said, "Woman was God's failure to make man". The old Welch law gave man the right to beat his wife with a broom stick on any part of the body except the head.

Socrates, one of the so-called wise men of his day, said that he was grateful to the gods for three things:

1. He was thankful that he was a Greek and not
   a Barbarian
2. He was a freeman and not a slave
3. He was a man and not a woman

If a man desired to sell his wife, then he could do so for the slightest cause. If he desired to buy her back out of the slave market, then he could do so for as little as fifty cents. None of the rights of men as free men were accorded the women. As the Christian religion has made its way into the hearts of men, women have been set free. Paul was right when he said, "There is neither male nor female but all are one in Christ Jesus."

THERE ARE STILL MANY PLACES WHERE WOMANHOOD NEEDS TO BE SET FREE

In many areas of the world people are bound down by superstitions. There was an old saying, "He who talks with a woman is qualifying for hell." Polygamy is practiced. Morals are at a low ebb. Children are born but are not wanted by many who bear them. There is joy when a boy is born, while the coming of a girl baby is not to be rejoiced over. In India there are more than 600,000 widows under nineteen years of age. There are more than 200,000 under fourteen. There are 78,000 under nine years of age. The cruel caste system forbids the remarriage of these (unless this has been changed in recent years).

If the Christian religion did nothing more than free people from their superstitions among suffering womanhood then the spirit of humanitarianism would compel us to continue to win these from their ignorance and superstition. Since God in Christ has done so much for women, they in turn are eternally indebted to honor Christ in all areas of life.

THE ENGLISH SPEAKING PEOPLE HAVE BEEN
SLOW TO LEARN

There have been laws that have allowed men to beat their wives and to put them away for almost any trivial act. If woman cooked her husband's food badly or salted it too much, then if he desired he could put her away. If he saw another fairer than his wife he could put her away and get another. Now, it seems that both man and woman can put the other away if he or she so desires. This is one of the failures of mankind. Men and women have failed in their marriage vows when they feel that they are free to put a companion aside for almost any reason and choose another. The Bible places certain restrictions upon those who enter into a marriage relationship. The marriage contract is too easily broken by people who have entered into so vital a relationship. Jesus had profound respect for women.

The disciples of Jesus would have passed the woman of Samaria by! But Jesus would not pass her by for he saw within her a need for that which he could give. The woman was amazed at the breach of custom on the part of this man whom she knew not but presently she was to come into a vital and a living relationship with the Son of God.

JESUS ALWAYS LIFTS AND EXALTS
WOMANHOOD WHEN GIVEN A CHANCE

Jesus and Jesus alone can and will present woman at her best. When women trust in Christ and live for him then they are a treasure and not a toy or a plaything. She is man's equal and not his slave. When Christ is magnified in the heart and life of a woman then she becomes a blessing in the home and out in the busy marts of trade. Man is no longer superior to woman when both are within the Kingdom of our Lord. The Apostle Paul makes a profound statement when he said, "For ye are all the children of God by faith in Christ Jesus." Again

34

he says, "There is neither Jew nor Greek, there is neither male nor female: for ye are all one in Christ Jesus." Civilization will rise or fall with womanhood. When women stoop to the low standards of men, then we are doomed.

WOMAN'S PLACE IN SOCIETY

Within the lifetime of many of us women have come out of the home into public life. Woman is a help-meet, a home builder, and a teacher. So much of the religious life in the family is left up to the mother. If the mothers fail, the loss will be irreparable. Women occupy a most prominent place in the business and educational world. Most of the young people enrolled in our colleges are women. Most of the public school teachers are women. Many of our missionaries, Christian workers, and church workers are women. In the Christian religion women brought to this work the comradeship, companionship, and fellowship that she could share with others. She indeed is a co-worker and a true yokefellow in God's work. Our women have made and are making a distinct contribution to Christianity. Since Jesus has done so much for women it is only fair and just that they devote their best talents to Him and to His work. Christian womanhood can help to make the future safe as they give themselves to making the home truly Christian. We will not have better homes until we have within them better people than many of them are today.

LOOK AT SOME OF THE GODLY
MOTHERS OF THE BIBLE

Not too many mothers of men are pointed out as worthy of our emulation. However, we have several examples of good and God-fearing women who made a distinct contribution to the society in which they lived in their day.

Hannah was a godly mother. She was a good mother. She

was a woman of great faith. When according to nature she could not have, neither would she ever bear, a son, God assured her that she would have a son. She claimed this promise. She took her burden and her concern to God. 1 Samuel 1:10-19. Before Samuel was born she dedicated him to God. She honored God in her walk and in her life. Such a mother merits the honor of her family. God give us more mothers like Hannah and more Christian homes.

Joccabed was a godly mother. She was honored with three noble children. Moses, Miriam, and Aaron each made a very distinct contribution to the people of God. When God needed a man to be the deliverer, leader and lawgiver He chose Moses. The most important teaching in the life of Moses came from his mother. In the crisis hour God needed a good and a well trained man. Moses was His man! "And Moses was learned in all the wisdom of the Egyptians, and honored this mother in that He chose Moses as the man of the hour."

Jedidah was also a godly mother. Not much was said about this mother. We find that she had her problems in life. Most mothers do have their problems. Being the wife of a king presented many problems. She had the problem of having a wicked husband. This made it more difficult to make the home what it should have been. Amon her husband and his father Mannasseh were wicked men. Fortunately for Jedidah her husband died young. She lived in a day and time when there was great wickedness in the land. In making a godly home this mother met with many outside forces that tended to destroy that which she sought to teach her son. It is said of Josiah, "And he did that which was right in the sight of the Lord, and walked in all the way of David his father, and turned not aside to the right hand or to the left." II Kings 22:2 The mother of Josiah was rewarded for her faithfulness. She did not shift her responsibility to servants.

36

She gave her best to her son and to his training. Her son was an honor to her worthy example.

Elizabeth was a godly woman. She was chosen to be the mother of John the Baptist, the fore-runner of Jesus who was chosen to be the Savior of the world. God needs good women, and God-fearing women to be the mothers of great men. She walked in the ordinances and commandments of the Lord. She was a faithful worshipper of God. She was blameless before the Lord. She and her good life were projected through her noble son. Both parents of John were God-fearing people. "And they were both righteous before God, walking in all the commandments and ordinances of the Lord, blameless." Luke 1:6. It is in the plan of God that children have the tender care and keeping of a godly mother and a godly father. Blessed is that child entrusted to parents who love, serve, and honor God. It is said of John before he was born: "For he shall be great in the sight of the Lord, and shall drink neither wine nor strong drink; and he shall be filled with the Holy Spirit, even from his mother's womb." Luke 1:15. One of the great needs of this day is for more parents who have deep convictions as to what is right over against that which is wrong.

Mary, the mother of Jesus, was a godly woman. She was chosen to give birth to God's only begotten Son because of her fitness as a Virgin. The Bible tells us that "the virgin's name was Mary". An angel came to Mary and told her that she was to be highly honored by God. She had found favor with God. The angel said to Mary, "And behold thou shalt conceive in thy womb, and bring forth a son, and shalt call his name Jesus." Luke 1:31. When this news came to Mary she exclaimed, "My soul doth magnify the Lord. My spirit hath rejoiced in God my Savior." We can safely say that Mary did her best with her son to do that which would be pleasing to God. She gave herself to the making of a God honoring

37

home. As other children came to bless the home this wonderful mother gave attention to their spiritual well-being, too.

HONOR TO WHOM HONOR IS DUE!

One is not to be honored just because he or she is a father or a mother. Often a child will say, "How can I honor my father when I know he is a crook?" The daughter may ask, "How can I honor and respect my mother when I know that she is leading a sinful and unclean life?" It is true that we are commanded to love and to honor our parents. If we are to do this, then our parents should be people who honor God in the highest sense. Deserving honor is a most noble thing. In the home where Christ is magnified by mother and by father, it is reasonable to expect that the children too will honor and fear God. It is easy to honor those who are worthy because of who they are as Christian men and women. What a privilege it is to be a parent! What a joy it should be for us to give Christ his rightful place in all of our activities! He merits the chief place in every mother's heart and home. To help make the home Christian is a high privilege that rests heavily upon mother and father. In working together they can realize the desires of their hearts. Young mothers would do well to ponder the wisdom recorded in Proverbs 31 where many great and good things are spoken about the "Prudent Mother".

CHAPTER FOUR

A FATHER'S DAY MESSAGE
2 Samuel 18:19-33

The story of David and the death of his son Absalom depicts the relationship of father and son in the King's family. It is a story filled with heart-break and deep regrets. David asked of the messengers who came with news about the King's son, "Is the young man Absalom safe?" Since this son had led a rebellion against his father and was now dead there was a feeling that the King would rejoice in this. However, when he was told of the tragedy he cried out, "O my son Absalom, my son, my son Absalom! Would God I had died for thee, O Absalom, my son, my son!" The king had gone into his private chamber where he, almost overcome with emotion, wept because of the death of his son. It seems to me that I have seen many parents along through the years who became concerned too late about the well-being of their children. They wake up, but too late. There is a time in the lives of children when if they are neglected by parents, the loss is irrevocable. We should hear and heed the words of the Apostle Paul who said, "Awake thou that sleepest and arise from the dead and Christ shall give thee light . . . ."

It has been my privilege to belong to several civic clubs. It has interested me to observe how anxious many have been about 100 percent attendance records and how these same members will make special effort when visiting in another city to make up their attendance. Often these men are church men with families and yet they do not have the same degree of loyalty to their church. They do not strive to make a perfect record at church with their children who need the influence and direction offered by the church.

NOTE SOME THINGS ABOUT THIS FATHER

David was a great man. He was king. He was a man in whose record there are many wonderful things recorded. There was a period in his life when he was a man "after God's own heart". This could have been true all the way through his life, but it was not. If you will read the history of King David you will find that there are few who compare favorably with him. As a shepherd lad he followed and trusted God. Many of his Psalms reflect this fact. There was a time when he had a personal encounter with God. The first and twenty-third Psalms depict this. During the early years of his reign he had close fellowship with God. These were seventeen years of great prosperity for David and for the people of God. It was at the height of his prosperity that he drifted away from God and fell into sin. Would it not have been wonderful if this chapter in his life had not been written?

David sowed "wild oats". One of the great laws in life, "whatsoever a man soweth that shall he also reap", is found in the Bible. Often people fail to ponder this inescapable law of life. Other laws that man cannot destroy are — be sure your sins will find you out, and the wages of sin is death. These laws hold true even though a man may deny the Bible. How true is the Proverb — "There is a way that seemeth right unto a man but the end thereof are the ways of death . . . ." No sensible person would sow as many are doing if they

40

could see the bitter harvest which they shall have to reap somewhere along the way. If you will but trace the acts of David you will find that for every sin he committed there was a time when he sowed the seed that brought forth this harvest. So often families are lost because parents have gone back on God and have drifted into sin. They have become wicked, wayward, drifting, and indifferent toward God. In the hour of deep grief and sorrow David wished that he had died instead of his son Absalom. He woke up, but he woke up too late.

At a time when David's children needed him the most he was concerned with other things. It seemed that the duties of the kingdom and social affairs claimed much of the time and attention of the King. We can become over-absorbed in our duties in business. We can be too concerned with social engagements, even to the neglect of the most important things in life. No person who has assumed the responsibilites of being father or mother should fail their child or children. The duties of proper teaching and counseling the members of the family are set forth in Deuteronomy 6. David had learned this passage when a child. Somehow David had neglected and drifted away from the basic principles learned in youth. Is this not true of many of us today? David was under obligation to God "to teach these things diligently unto thy children . . . ." When we search the scriptures we find that some other great and good men neglect their families for things of lesser importance. Often good people neglect their children while they are concerned about important matters that are within the range of their obligations. Samuel, as good and fine as he was, neglected his own children. Many times pastors neglect their children while they are preaching to others. In 1st Samuel 4th chapter we read the story of Eli and his tragic failure with his own sons. On every hand we, too, can see the tragic results of the neglect of moral and spiritual things. This is true not only in a family, but in nations as well.

David's sin was the sin of the busy man. He was not accused of being lazy or idle. While he was absorbed in the duties of King and the social activities in the palace he lost his best chance with his sons.

Every father should take time out to play with his children, to counsel them, and to share in their problems and their plans for the future. Too many fathers are so busy that when the child comes to him with some joy or sorrow, he is turned aside with the old saying "go away and don't bother me, I am busy". Has it ever occured to you that some of your time belongs to your family? In I Kings 20:35-43 there is a very interesting story of a man who was entrusted with a prisoner to guard and to keep. If the guard should for any reason let this man entrusted to him escape then his life or payment in silver would be required. He failed in the trust that was committed to him. The prisoner did escape. The guard's answer to his failure to keep a close eye on the man was, "And as thy servant was busy here and there he was gone." You will observe that the man was not asleep. He was not idle. While he was busy he neglected to guard carefully the man who was left in his custody. Fathers, we can be busy, and busy with good and important things, but fail our children. If we fail them then we condemn ourselves.

Greatness

A father is as great as the dreams he dreams;
As great as the love he bears;
As great as values he redeems,
And the happiness he shares.
A father is as great as the thoughts he thinks;
As the worth he has attained;
As the fountains at which his spirit drinks,
And the insight he has gained.

A father is as great as the help he gives,
As great as the destiny he seeks;
As great as the life he lives.

Adapted

SOME OF THE RESULTS OF
THE SIN OF THE BUSY MAN

Absalom rebelled against his father. "He stole the hearts of the people." For two years Absalom did not visit his father even though they lived in the same city. He had the barley fields of Joab destroyed. He was the moving spirit in a plot to get rid of his own father. The king cried out, "Behold my son seeketh my life." Some of the things perpetrated by Absalom and his cohorts sound like events during the reign of Henry the 8th. Absalom lacked a moral and a spiritual foundation upon which to build. What a picture of someone's tragic failure!

Father and son met after a period of silence of two years. They kissed and seemed to make up. They went through a form of forgiveness. Nothing is so bitter as a family fuss. It tends to destroy every fiber of love and devotion. The kingdom was divided because the King's family was divided. Many found it difficult to decide which side to take. As a result of this trouble in the King's household 20,000 people were slain in one day. Many more were devoured in the woods. The kingdom was torn with strife from one end to the other. Absalom was slain. David was greatly troubled and grieved. This tragic situation followed David to his grave. He woke up too late. He became concerned when it was too late.

WE NEED TO HAVE CONCERN FOR OUR FAMILIES

Real deep and abiding concern for the spiritual welfare of our homes is urgently needed today. Paul had concern for his own people. "Brethren, my heart's desire and prayer to God for Israel is that they might be saved." He also said he could wish himself accursed from God for his own people. It seems that we are more concerned about material prosperity than we are about the moral and spiritual health of our loved ones. We could well ask, What shall a family be profited if that family should have wealth, social prestige, fame, fortune, and power and lack security in Christ? God has invested certain powers and responsibilities in parents. We must not fail God. He is counting upon us. We will have to give an account to God for what we do with that which has been committed to us. How true it is, "That no man liveth to himself and no man dieth to himself." So many homes that are broken today could have been saved if father and mother had accepted the task and privilege of making a house a home. How can our children honor us when we fail to honor God? David asked too late, "Is my son Absalom safe?" The story of the Shunamite family is a most striking one. The mother was asked, "Is it well with thee? Is it well with the father? Is it well with the son?" Yes, it was well, and it was well because each member of the family was anchored in God. Even though the son was dead it was well because he was saved. Had he not been saved all would not have been well with this family.

It seems to me that when Enoch faced the fact that he was to become a father he gave serious consideration to his relationship to God. Somewhere in the days as he looked for the coming of his son, Methuselah, he put his faith in God. Near the end of his journey it is said, "And Enoch walked with God: and he was not; for God took him," Genesis 5:24

GOD BLESS OUR FATHERS

It is true that many fathers are not worthy of the honor of being called father. We speak often of juvenile problems. This is sadly true. However, on the other hand we have problem parents. J. Edgar Hoover spoke a great truth when

44

he said, "Parents are not enough to cope with the problems of today." We need all the help we can command in our efforts to do a good job in guiding our children across the perilous sea of life which is fraught with perils, problems, pitfalls, and dangerous influences that we must encounter. We must not forget the God-honoring and God-fearing fathers who give themselves sacrificially to their families. They give their children a good start in life because of what they are in character. They help to create a good and safe environment in which to grow. They give their sons and daughters wise counsel and help. Many fathers make great sacrifices in providing for their children. They labor long and hard to give them the things needed physically, mentally, morally and spiritually. Often fathers deny themselves many good things in order that those they love may have advantages which they never knew. We bless the memory of our fathers because of the good example they left us. We cherish the memory of fathers because of the wise and safe counsel which they gave us. We are eternally grateful to our fathers for the provision they made for our physical needs. If you will search the records you will find that most of our missionaries, pastors, and lay leaders come from homes where the fathers have been faithful in the performance of their duties as spiritual patriarchs. If our fathers are honorable and faithful in making the home truly Christian then we can with ease, respect, honor and reverence them. God grant that more sons and daughters shall have the wonderful inheritance that comes because of the man whom they call father.

God, Give Us Men

God give us men —
Men of courage and strong,
Who know God's sacred truth
And hold it fast against
    All subtle doubt

45

Their faith to flout.
God give us men —
Men who love their Lord,
Who bear His cross, upheld
By faith in Him for whom
        They scorn the hour
        Of error's power.
God give us men —
Men who guard the right
Oppose the wrong; although
It cost them grievous loss
        And travail long,
        They march right on.
God give us men —
Men who stand foursquare
For all the work of Christ,
Men high of heart and soul
        Who shun no text
        To serve Christ best.
God give us men —
Times like these require
Great men in whom there dwells
The holy Spirit, who
        Gives God's light
        Against man's night.
God give us men —
Issacharian men,
Who understand the times
And know full well God's call —
        The truth to sound.
        The world around.

                                    Selected

CHAPTER FIVE

THE LIGHT OF FREEDOM
(July 4th message)

"Then said Jesus to those Jews who believed on him, If ye continue in my word, then are ye my disciples indeed;

And ye shall know the truth, and the truth shall make you free." John 8:31-32

Freedom is the inalienable right of every person. We are a part of a world that is part slave and part free. Many people are never free from fear, want, hunger, war, poverty, and oppression. The over-whelming mass of mankind has never known the true meaning of freedom. Our own United States of America is thought of as the freest land in all the world. Standing in the New York harbor is the Statue of Liberty. As one stands before it he can read these immortal words:

"Give me your tired, your poor,
Your huddled masses yearning to breathe free,
The wretched refuge of your teeming shore.
Send these, the homeless, the tempest-tost, to me:
I lift my lamp beside the golden door."

In the great cosmopolitan population of our country many have come from lands of persecution and oppression seeking freedom. They enjoy breathing the fresh and invigorating atmosphere of freedom. Many have learned to

47

sing and love the Battle Hymn of the Republic.

> "In the beauty of the lilies Christ was born across the
> sea,
> With a glory in his bosom that transfigures you and
> me;
> As He died to make men holy let us die to make men
> free;
> While God is marching on.
> Glory, glory, Hallelujah, His truth is marching on."

Let us hope that those who think of America as the great Bulwark of Freedom will not be disappointed. The words on the Liberty Bell are found in Leviticus 25:10. They are as follows, "Proclaim liberty throughout all the land, unto all the inhabitants thereof." No person can enjoy the finest freedom until he has been set free from sin by the great and eternal emancipator, Christ Jesus.

THE MEANING OF FREEDOM

In the Bill of Rights we are guaranteed the Freedom of Assembly, the Freedom of Speech, the Freedom of Press, and the Freedom of Religion. Certain rights and responsibilities are involved in freedom. If each one becomes a law unto himself and does not respect the rights of others, this leads to anarchy. When we do not respect the rights of others we violate their rights. Some one has rightfully said, "Liberty is not the right to do what you choose; it is the responsiblity of choosing to do what is right." The Scripture enjoins us, "Use not your liberty as an occasion of the flesh . . . . ." To become a law unto yourself leads to license, and fails to recognize that your freedom ends where the rights of the other person begins. Some of the most violent crimes have been committed within recent years in the name of freedom. All of this adds up to anarchy. It violates the civil and the spiritual rights of others. Those who are free and would

48

continue to be free should respect the rights of others, whether they be property rights, personal rights, or religious views that are contrary to his. Great inalienable rights are guaranteed to each and to all in the Constitution of the United States. These rights must be defended and protected.

Some do not realize that freedom has restraints. It also means that certain responsibilities rest upon the free. Abraham Lincoln said, "In giving freedom to the slave we assume freedom to the free." Each citizen in a free country is assured of his rights. He should seek to make his country strong and not help to destroy the right of any man. A man driving down a highway has a right to do so, and is given a license to drive. However, others have that right also. Each driver should respect the rights of every other driver. When we fail to do so, and drive on the wrong side of the highway, or drive drunk, or recklessly, and an accident occurs then we have failed to respect and safe-guard the rights of another. The torch of Freedom's Light should be held high by each person who walks in the light of that freedom.

FREEDOM HAS BEEN PURCHASED AT A GREAT PRICE

> "My country tis of thee, sweet land of liberty,
> Of thee I sing;
> Land where my fathers died,
> Land of the pilgrim's pride,
> From every mountain side,
> Let freedom ring."

Some seem to forget the price that was paid for the freedom which is ours. It was handed down to those who wrought well, and fought heroically for the right to be free. The signing of the Declaration of Independence was proceeded by grave and trying conditions. This eventful day could not have been, had it not been for the sacrifice of our founding fathers. It is not enough for our freedom to have been won. It could be lost in any age. We should therefore do what we can to protect and to defend our freedom. It has been said, "Eternal vigilance is the price of liberty."

SOME FACTS THAT HISTORY RECORDS

When the Declaration was signed in 1776 the Negroes were still slaves. However, in a later date the Emancipation Proclamation was signed by President Lincoln and the Negroes were set free.

Baptist people played a big part in getting Article VI written into the Constitution. It reads as follows, "Congress shall make no laws respecting the establishment of religion, or prohibiting the free exercise thereof, or abridging the freedom of speech, or of the press, or the right of the people to peaceably assemble and petition the government for a redress of grievances." This was written and passed while Mr. Madison was President in 1789.

John Locke said, "The Baptists were the first propounders of absolute liberty, equal and impartial liberty, in the United States."

Dr. E. Y. Mullins said, "Baptists gave to American civilization the complete idea of liberty."

"Among the Baptists, Christian freedom found its earliest, its staunchest, its most consistent, and its most interested champions. Not less powerful has been the influence of Baptists in the United States. Persecuted themselves, they never persecuted others. The paths of the Baptists are the paths of freedom, pleasantness, and peace."

(Appleton's American Encyclopedia,
Volume II, Page 293)

According to history all states persecuted others for having differing views on religion except Rhode Island and Pennsylvania. The other eleven states had the established church. Baptists were not allowed to vote because they did not belong to the established church. Patrick Henry defended a Baptist minister who was haled into court. In his defense he said, "Gentlemen of the jury, this man is charged with preaching the glorious Gospel of Jesus Christ."

Some people are willing to tolerate others but are not willing to give them the same liberty and freedom they claim for themselves. "Toleration is a concession while liberty is the inherent right of a person. Toleration is a gift from man, while liberty is a gift from God."

America gave to the world the best example of liberty and freedom. Thomas Jefferson worked 18 days on the writing of the Declaration of Independence. Benjamin Franklin and John Adams added their suggestions. Congress cut out and added some things. This document guarantees to all citizens of this country "Life, Liberty and the Pursuit of Happiness".

Many times our liberties become imperiled. The strength of our democracy is in the fact that each person is regarded as free, and yet that strong point could be our destruction as a free people. Civil liberties are assured in the constitution. Soul liberty can only be assured by our Maker, God himself. History proves that Christianity fares best under the democratic form of government.

A WARNING

In a New York paper some years ago a French laborer was quoted as saying: "We were defeated because we came to imagine that the proper duty of man was to arrange an easy way of life, individualistic to the point of selfishness. We saw no further than the village pump. We looked upon the state as a universal purveyor, and we always spoke of our due, seldom of our duties. We imagined that the state was a milk cow. Tell this to the Americans and warn them at the same time of the peril that may befall democracy everywhere

51

when we forget that free men have duties as well as rights."
In the light of this statement consider the face that some
people in our day advocate that the government feed people
who can work, and pay them a stated salary while they do
not work, when these same people often create riots and
destroy that which belongs to the government or private
individuals.

WE SHOULD SHARE THE BLESSINGS
WHICH ARE OURS AS FREE MEN

Many people in the world are enslaved by disease,
poverty, and ignorance. Millions of people go to bed hungry
every night. We should do what we can to relieve the fear of
starvation. There are more kinds of slavery than that of being
subject to some master who owns one. In many countries
man is a tool. He is subject to a totalitarian form of
government. He does not enjoy the freedom and the dignity
accorded man in a free state.

Jesus in speaking to believing Jews reminded them that if
they would continue in His word, then they would be true
disciples. He assured them that the truth would be known
and that that truth would make them free. No man will be
truly free until his sins are all forgiven and he comes under
the Mastery of Jesus Christ who makes people free indeed.

SOUL LIBERTY

Soul liberty is a fundamental principle emphasized in the
Bible. Each person is responsible to God for what he does or
does not do in the light of the revealed and inspired Word of
God. Each one of us must account to God. There can be no
proxy in religion. Many have been taught that parents can
answer to God for the children. Each person must account to
God for himself. He is free when God's purpose is being
realized in his life. Someone has said, "There are three levels

52

of freedom. They are the superficial, the conditional, and the basal. The first is a matter of taste. The second is a matter of circumstance. The third is a matter of essence. I am free when I am fully myself, when God's purpose is realized in my life." Often we confuse independence with freedom. No person is absolutely independent of other people. We are inter-dependent. No person really lives unto himself. Some confuse autonomy with freedom and liberty. When you are tempted to think of the autonomy of a democratic body, do not forget the privilege and responsibility that is yours to work within the framework of like bodies that are autonomous. A free church, in a free state, in a free society is to be desired. God is the true author of Liberty and freedom. His Word is the true light of freedom.

The scripture enjoins us — "Stand fast therefore in the liberty wherewith Christ hath made us free, and be not entangled again with the yoke of bondage . . . For, brethren, ye have been called unto liberty; only use not liberty as an occasion to the flesh, but by love serve one another." Galatians 5:1, 13. Jesus said, "If the Son therefore shall make you free, ye shall be free indeed." John 8:36

True soul liberty means that any and all shall have the right to worship or not to worship as they may choose to so do. This is a basic right. Man in his natural state is a sinner. He is in bondage. Only the power of God can break the bondage of sin and set a man free. Many people who have fought for freedom and the cause of liberty have been enslaved by lust, passions, and evil desires. Man is not able to free himself from the enslavement of sin. A man can have liberty and freedom of soul even in prison. We have only to read of how John Bunyan stayed in jail at Bedford, England rather than to make a slaughter house of his convictions and conscience. Paul and Silas had soul freedom in jail. So did Peter and John. Where God's Spirit is within the heart and

53

soul of man there is liberty, there is life, there is light, there is love, and there is likeness. 2 Corinthians 3:17-18. Surely every Christian should hold high the Light of Freedom.

CHAPTER SIX

THE GRACE OF GRATITUDE
(A THANKSGIVING MESSAGE)

"In everything give thanks: for this is the will of God in Christ Jesus concerning you." 1 Thessalonians 5:18

For many people this art and grace of gratitude is real. It is given much attention in their lives. For others it is an unknown art. The note of praise is sounded in many places in the Bible. The Psalms resound with thanksgiving and grateful acknowledgement of God's goodness and blessings. We should emphasize the note of thanks in family life. Children should be taught to say, "Thank you Mother for the good meal." "Thank you Daddy for your love and care." In everything give thanks for this is the will of God for you. To express our gratitude to those who bless us in so many ways is a good medicine for us and for those to whom we give our thanks. Only one day is set aside as Thanksgiving Day but every day should be a thanksgiving day. In fact this is the will of God for us. We are to thank God for who He is, and for what He does for us. Not all people can truly be thankful for they know not God. Some who do know Him fail to offer to Him daily their thanks.

CONSIDER SOME WHO ARE NOT THANKFUL
The agnostic cannot be thankful. He knows no God to

whom he is indebted for the blessings bestowed upon mankind daily. The atheist cannot be grateful for he does not believe in a living and a beneficent God. The materialist cannot be thankful for he does not give God the honor and credit for life's blessings and gifts. Such a one gives undue credit to his own skill and ingenuity. The man who lives by the philosophy of the Epicurean cannot be grateful for he does not think of life as reaching beyond this brief span that we call life on earth. He lives with the feeling that one should eat, drink, and enjoy life now for tomorrow he may be dead, and that is the end of life. To express our thanks puts us under obligation to God. It tends to save us from pride, arrogancy, and ourselves.

THERE ARE WAYS WHEREBY WE CAN EXPRESS OUR GRATITUDE

Thank you is a welcomed word in any and all languages. It brings a smile on the face of the stranger. People who travel extensively learn several words that mean Thank You. There is a proverb which says, "A word fitly spoken is like apples of gold in pictures of silver." Proverbs 25:11. In words we can express our appreciation to people. To begin a day with gratitude in the heart will make a big difference. There are many, many people who need a lift. A word fitly spoken may change the whole day for some person who has problems and difficulties too heavy to be borne. Too many people live on "Grumbler's Row". If we could have just one day in the year in which to do all of our grumbling what a blessed thing this might prove to be. If on that day we could just think of everything that we would like to grumble about — and get it out of our systems — and live the rest of the year with the grace of gratitude glowing and growing, surely God would be pleased and those whose lives we touch would be better by the touch. Life is either a howl or a song.

WE CAN EXPRESS OUR THANKS IN OUR
DEEDS AND WORKS

We are to "serve the Lord with gladness". In Psalm 116 a very profound question is asked — "What shall I render unto the Lord for all his benefits toward me?" It seems that the answer to this question could be found in doing at least four things that will be well pleasing to God. In taking the cup of salvation, in calling upon the name of the Lord, in paying vows to God, and offering the sacrifices of thanksgiving; the psalmist says he can express his thanks and gratitude to God for "all his benefits".

THE SIN OF INGRATITUDE AND A LESSON
IN GRATITUDE
Luke 17:11-19

Jesus illustrates how some Jews called upon him for mercy. He heard their cry and healed their leprous bodies. One in the group was a Samaritan, a man ordinarily despised by the Jews. No doubt those who were healed were very happy that their bodies were cleansed. The Samaritan was not only happy but was grateful for that which had come to him. He turned back and "glorified God . . . and fell down on his face at his feet, giving him thanks; and he was a Samaritan." Jesus was concerned about the nine that were cleansed and went on their merry way. He asked, "Were there not ten cleansed? But where are the nine?" In thanking Jesus a greater blessing was in store for the grateful man. Jesus said to him, "Arise and go thy way: thy faith hath made thee whole."

"Are you ever burdened with a load of care?
Does the cross seem heavy you are called to bear?
Count your many blessings every doubt will fly
And you will be singing as the days go by."

So often we get the least from those from whom the

most should be expected. On the other hand we often get the most from those of whom we expect the least. Not long ago I read the story of a birthday party given for an elderly woman who was celebrating her 90th. birthday. The baker at the hotel who had baked many cakes baked a beautiful cake for her. After the party the old lady wrote the baker and thanked him for such a good cake. She enclosed a $5.00 bill as a small token of her gratitude. He in turn came to see her and to thank her for the note and the gift. This was the first time in all of his career of baking cakes that anyone had ever thanked him for baking a cake. He had been taken for granted too long. Often we take people who do the most for us for granted.

LIFE'S BLESSINGS FOR WHICH WE SHOULD BE GRATEFUL

Every day we enjoy physical blessings for which we are thankful. It is possible to be thankful even though certain afflictions have been laid upon us. Many times God has some great hidden blessings in affliction. A helpless and almost hopeless crippled woman was asked how she could be so cheerful in the face of her physical infirmities. She replied in the words of Psalm 103: "Bless the Lord, O my soul: and all that is within me, bless his holy name. Bless the Lord, O my soul, and forget not all his benefits: who forgiveth all thine iniquities; who healeth all thy diseases; who redeemeth thy life from destruction; who crowneth thee with loving kindness and tender mercies; who satisfieth thy mouth with good things; so that thy youth is renewed like the eagle's."

We should be thankful for material blessings. We are reminded over and over again that all good gifts come from God. To receive God's blessings daiiy should make us feel that we are indebted to God for such. It should be a joy and a delight to give him thanks. The story is told of a free and abundantly flowing spring by the side of a road. Some one had placed this sign at the spring, "Praise me by drinking".

We should be grateful for the spiritual blessings that come to us. Such blessings are to be personally appropriated. We are to enjoy such blessings. We are to unfold them and share them with others.

We teach people a little chorus which expresses our thanks to God for salvation.

"Thank you Lord for saving my soul,
Thank you Lord for making me whole,
Thank you Lord for giving to me
Thy great salvation so full and free."

Someone has said "Gratitude is the smile of faith as she looks into the face of grace, and when that is absent our religious service is barren indeed." We should have joy in saying, "Thanks be unto God for his unspeakable gift." 2 Corinthians 9:15. Then, too, we should joy in the assurance that God's greatest gift assures us victory. "But thanks be to God, who giveth us the victory through our Lord Jesus Christ." 1 Corinthians 15:57. God's greatest gift to us was that of His son. This should evoke eternal gratitude from every Christian. "For God so loved the world that he gave his only begotten son that whosoever believeth on him should not perish but have everlasting life." John 3:16

COUNT THE OTHER BLESSINGS TOO

Many good things come to us because we are a part of a good family. There are opportunities of worship and services in our churches where we belong. There are pastors, teachers, musicians, and others who help in making living worth the while. We are in a country where God has bestowed many wonderful blessings within the area of freedom. We take these, too often, for granted. These freedoms have come to us because of the sacrifices of those who "blazed the trail" through the wilderness. There are also institutions that contribute to our well-being. How many of us praise and love our country. How many of us fail to measure up to the common everyday standards of good citizenship? We ask God to bless this, our land, and he has and does. How grateful are we for this land in which we live and share in her benefits and blessings?

> "My Country, 'tis of thee,
> Sweet land of liberty, of thee I sing:
> Land where my fathers died,
> Land of the pilgrim's pride,
> From every mountain side
> Let freedom ring!"

S. F. Smith

CHAPTER SEVEN

THE MEANING OF CHRISTMAS
(A CHRISTMAS MESSAGE)

The greatest and most thrilling news ever heard was announced by an angel who said, "Fear not for, behold, I bring you good tidings of great joy, which shall be to all people. For unto you is born this day in the city of David a Savior, who is Christ the Lord." Luke 2:10-11

Old Testament prophets foretold the coming of a Savior. Many had been looking for the coming of the Messiah. The time had come for the fulfillment of God's divine promises. He had come to be a Savior to all of those who hopefully had been looking for Him. He had come to save from their sins all who were willing to trust Him.

Believer and unbeliever take note of Christmas. Many have turned Christmas into a highly commercialized season. It is easy for people to get lost in the bright glitter and glow of tinsel and various kinds of decorations. We hear the old familiar songs which are meaningful for many, while to others they are meaningless. We send and we receive cards with such greetings as "Merry Christmas", "Have a Good Christmas", "Wishing for you all the joy the season brings", and other familiar phrases.

In speaking of Christmas and the spirit of Christmas we

61

do not all mean the same thing. For some it is a time of revelry. Many celebrate by drinking and over-eating. There are so many who spend recklessly and wastefully.

Then there are those who really make this season of the year meaningful. Families get together and enjoy the renewed fellowship in the family. The blessings of God are reviewed and are gratefully acknowledged. The getting together of families brings back many memories. Many people recognize that if Christ is left out of the celebrations of this season it is really not a Christ honoring occasion. To have a worship service at Christmas is altogether in keeping with the true spirit of Christmas.

LET US CONSIDER THE FIRST CHRISTMAS

The place is Bethlehem. This had been foretold by the prophets. Can you recall your first Christmas, where it was, who was present, and the gifts, even though simple, you enjoyed and appreciated?

The scene was in a manger. It was here that heaven and earth met. "And lo, the star which they saw in the east went before them til it came and stood over where the young child was. When they saw the star, they rejoiced with exceeding great joy." Matthew 2:9-10

The shepherds were in the field. The shepherds no doubt were looking for and longing for the coming of a Savior.

"And lo, the angel of the Lord came upon them, and the glory of the Lord shone round about them and they were sore afraid. And the angel said unto them, Fear not: for, behold, I bring you good tidings of great joy, which shall be too all people. For unto you is born this day in the city of David a Savior, which is Christ the Lord . . . And suddenly there was with the angel a multitude of the heavenly host praising God, and saying, Glory to God in the highest, and on earth peace, good will toward men." Luke 2:9-14

62

It is my conviction that the shepherds saw the Christ child and worshipped Him. They went on their ways "glorifying and praising God". It is natural to believe that they went on their ways rejoicing and telling others of this wonderful experience.

Some wise men from the east came to see this new born child. Matthew tells us that wise men came from the east to Jerusalem. They asked, "Where is he that is born king of the Jews that we may worship Him?" They had seen his star in the east and had followed it. They had come for the purpose of worshipping. Herod was troubled in soul when he heard about this promised King. His desire to see him was that he might destroy him. He instructed the wise men to come and tell him where the child was so that he too could "come and worship Him". The star stood over where the child lay in the manger. The wise men, we know not how many, rejoiced when they saw the star and felt that it had directed them to the right place and to the right child. "When they were come into the house, they saw the young child with Mary his mother, and fell down, and worshipped him: and when they had opened their treasures, they presented unto him gifts: gold, and frankincense, and myrrh." Matthew 2:11

It has been said that the wise men brought gold which symbolizes obedience. They brought frankincense which is symbolic of worship. They brought myrth which is a symbol of sacrifice.

Once a little girl gave a very precious gift. She was crippled, and had to use a crutch. She had nothing else to give so she gave her crutch. The church decided to give it back to her. She said, "I did not give it to you, but to Jesus."

There are two dangers that we must avoid in our day and time. In the first place we should honor Mary but never worship her. The wise men worshipped the Christ Child. The second error is to keep the babe in the manger and see only the baby Jesus. Jesus grew up and became a man and yet Very God. We are to worship the God-man. Too many people never get beyond the manger scene. We should see the Christ suffering and dying on the cross for sinners.

One of the old hymns expresses the thought and act of worship.

"O worship the king, all glorious above,
And gratefully sing his wonderful love:
Our shield and defender, the ancient of days,
Pavillioned in splendor, and girded with praise."

WE CAN MAKE CHRISTMAS MEANINGFUL

We can make Christmas meaningful if we give Christ His rightful place. For many He must be brought back and given the central place in their activities. This means that He must be first in religious life. It is not easy to tell a professed Christian from a non-professing Christian. So many pastors say that it is difficult to get people who are church members to attend worship at Christmas. We are so involved in the commerce and the "rush of Christmas" that we do not take time to worship. We sing "Living for Jesus" and often fail to interpret that song in everyday living. We sing "He Lives, He Lives, Christ Jesus lives today. You ask me how I know He lives, He lives within my heart." But people are still saying, "Sirs, we would see Jesus."

Jesus should be given first place in our social activities. There is no place for sinful indulgences at Christmas on the part of Christian people. If we are not Christian in our social activities then we are not truly Christian. Paul states a vital principle in 1 Corinthians 10:31: "Whether therefore ye eat, or drink, or whatsoever ye do, do all to the glory of God."

Can we truly sing:

"Were the whole realm of nature mine
That were a present far too small;

64

Love so amazing, so divine,
Demands my soul, my life, my all'"?

In the story of Joseph and Mary seeking a place in the Inn, it is said, "There was no room for him in the inn." That was indeed a sad picture. Yet, today so many people who profess to love Jesus with all of their faculties have crowded Him out. There is no room for Him in their activities.

WE ARE TO GIVE THIS MESSAGE
TO OTHERS

We have a message of good news. It would be sinful to hold this message. This is a day of good tidings and we should not keep it. We are to tell others what we have seen, heard and felt. The angels sounded the note of good news. So did the shepherds. So did the wise men. Would it not be glorious if all warring and fighting forces would join in singing, "Glory to God in the highest and peace on earth"?

Every person who has given Jesus his rightful place in heart and life can truly sing, "We've a story to tell to the nations that shall turn their hearts to the right." There will never be peace on earth and good will among men until they come to know the One who brings to the heart true peace. Jesus said, "My peace I leave with you, my peace I give unto you: not as the world giveth, give I unto you. Let not your heart be troubled, neither let it be afraid." John 14:27. Christmas is a good time for us to draw nigh to God. It is a good time to take stock and see if we are putting things in their right places and in their right relationship to other things. If those who do not know Christ as Savior and Lord will seek Him they can find Him. Those who sought Him on that first Christmas day found Him, for they had been seeking Him.

The story is told of an old man who sat on the street begging. He made a doleful sound with his old violin. He

65

hoped that the passersby would drop some coins into his almost empty cup. A very attractive young woman came that way. She asked the old man for his violin. As she played with the skill of a master violinist people were attracted. Soon the once empty cup was filled as this lovely young woman played, "Here Lord I give myself to thee, tis all that I can do."

In giving gifts at Christmas we should keep in mind that it is His birthday that we are celebrating. We should ask, What gift can I offer to Him that would please Him the most? He wants you. He is seeking for you. He is asking for your heart and life. He has made it possible for you to be in His fold as one of His sheep. He desires you. He has every right to possess you.

> "To give is to live,
> To deny is to die."

In John 1:11-12 is a picture of triumph and one of tragedy. Jesus was rejected by many. On the other hand He was accepted and trusted by others.

"He came unto his own and his own received him not. But as many as received him, to them gave he power to become the sons (children) of God, even to them that believe on his name:

Who were born, not of blood, nor of the will of the flesh, nor of the will of man, but of God."

There is a hymn which has in it words that are most fitting as we think of the Son of God being born of a Virgin but rejected by His own people. It is titled "Thou Didst Leave Thy Throne."

> "Thou didst leave thy throne
> And thy kingly crown,
> When thou camest to earth for me;
> But in Bethlehem's home
> Was there found no room,

For thy holy nativity.
Heaven's arches rang
When the angels sang
Proclaiming thy royal degree;
But of lowly birth
Didst Thou come to earth,
And in great humility.

Refrain:

O come to my heart Lord Jesus,
There is room in my heart for thee."

CHAPTER EIGHT

THE FINE ART OF WORSHIP

God has made man so that he craves and longs for fellowship with God. In his search for God man creates idols and gods to worship. The most primitive peoples, we find, have their places of worship. Altars are built and sacrifices are made to many and to various kinds of gods. All seek in their own way to find and worship the true God. Even those of us who know the true and the living God find it difficult to worship. Many have never known the fine art of woship. Many people think that attending one or more church services is to worship. In many of the prophetic messages in the Bible people were condemned for making offerings, sacrifices, but failing to truly worship God. "True worship must even be based upon recognition on the part of the worshipers of God's power and our dependence, or God's holiness and our sin, of God's grace and our gratitude." Dr. E. C. Dargan, preacher, writer, and theologian.

Several Greek words are used in reference to worship in the New Testament. The word "sebonai" means fear. Matthew 15:9. The prophet Isaiah says (Isaiah 29:13) "This people draw nigh unto me with their mouth, and with their lips do honor me; but have removed their heart far from me." Such people really do not worship God. They cannot until their hearts are made right with God. The word "latreuo" has reference to outward rites and ceremonies. Acts 7:42. The word "threskiea" refers to acts of worship. Colossians 2:18-19. There is the word "proskuneo" which means "to make obesience, or to prostrate oneself". Matthew 2:2. These four Greek words originally had reference to acts of worship which involved reverence for God and respect for man. What does the average church goer think is the deeper meaning of worship? When does one actually worship God?

THE UNIVERSAL NEED AND DESIRE
FOR WORSHIP

The need for worship is universal. Mankind has an inate desire to worship. It is true that man is restless until he finds rest in God. Our creator has thus made man. Augustine expressed it well when he said, "O Lord, thou hast made us for thyself, and our heart is restless until it repose in thee." This thought is found in Psalm 42:1-2. "As the heart panteth after the water brooks, so panteth my soul after thee, O God. My soul thirsteth for God, for the living God: when shall I come and appear before God?"

Because of man's needs that only can be met in true worship God has provided this opportunity for him. We are sinners and go astray. We sin and need to come to God for cleansing, for renewal, for strength. God seeks for man. Man is seeking for God. "My soul longeth for thee O God!", the Psalmist said. Again he said, "O come and let us worship and bow down . . ." Psalm 95:6 and "Exalt ye the Lord our God, and worship at his footstool: for He is holy." Psalm 99:5. If one will read Psalms 73 and 77 he will make some most interesting discoveries. He will find what happened to the Psalmist when he failed to worship God. He drifted away from God and became involved in wrong doing. Some serious doubts were raised in his mind. He wondered why the wicked

70

prospered. He had begun to feel that it did not pay to serve God. What a change came in his life when he returned to the sanctuary to confess his sins, forsake them and get right with God. No man can truly worship God who is out of fellowship with Him. We must first be made right with God, then can we worship Him in the beauty of holiness. In Acts 17 Paul is seeking to make known to people who worshipped a lifeless and helpless god the one true God who could meet their needs. These people had a desire for God. They had a burning need to know and to worship Him. "Whom therefore ye ignorantly worship, him declare I unto you", said Paul. Jesus said, "Thou shalt worship the Lord thy God, and him only shalt thou serve." Matthew 4:10. Any god is not as good as Jehovah God. There is but one true God.

PREPARING FOR WORSHIP

Preparation is a most vital and a most personal factor if public worship is to have vitality. Public worship will have power and meaning if and when the people have prepared for it. All of us know what it is to prepare our home for the coming of guests. Things are put in order and in their proper place. Dusting is done. If there are children then they, too, must be prepared for the coming of guests. If the guests are prominent people then some extra "doings" go on about the house. When I lived in the Southwest I would come home in the summer and spend about a month in the country with my parents. My mother usually had good chickens in readiness for us, along with other things. She had been thinking and planning ahead of time what she would do to make our visit enjoyable. She prepared. So did we prepare to enjoy our visit out in the open country.

Many of us know what it is to prepare on Saturday for worship on Sunday. My mother would prepare the clothes for the children. We would take our Saturday night baths. We

71

were told to study our Sunday School lessons. When Sunday arrived we would put on our Sunday best and go to church for worship. Physical preparation was just part of the picture. We would pray for the services, preacher, teachers, singers, and all who would meet for worship.

A very faithful and devout man said to his pastor, "I did not enjoy the sermon today." "Why?" asked the pastor. He answered, "I was so busy during the week until I did not take time to pray and to meditate before coming to church." Is this why so many of our services fail and fall short of the high purpose of worship? A congregation can make or ruin a service. We should prepare to worship by praying. "Wait on the Lord: be of good courage, and he shall strengthen thine heart: wait, I say, on the Lord." Psalm 27:14 "Who shall ascend into the hill of the Lord or who shall stand in his holy place? He that hath clean hands, and a pure heart; who hath not lifted up his soul unto vanity, nor sworn deceitfully." Psalm 24:3-4 "But they that wait upon the Lord shall renew their strength; they shall mount up with wings as eagles; they shall run, and not be weary; and they shall walk and not faint." Isaiah 40:31

If we prepare to worship, and are willing to give ourselves in worship in the service, we will receive a blessing as we are a blessing to others. We should attend worship services with a view to receiving some needed blessing. One of a certain preacher's critics said to the pastor one Lord's day, "Pastor, I never get anything out of your preaching." His reply was, "Sister, bring something to put it in."

The pastor should prepare for worship. This calls for mental, physical, and spiritual preparation. The God-called and anointed minister knows something of how essential it is for one to pray much as he seeks the will of God in selecting themes and preparing the sermons for the people who will be waiting upon his ministry. In the early church deacons were chosen to be helpers of the pastors. This was done so that the pastors could give themselves more completely to prayer and to the preaching of the Word. To fail in bringing the Lord's messages to His people is a colossal failure. It is almost unforgivable for a man of God to fail in preparing fully for His divinely appointed task. To lead people in worship, in soul searching, and God honoring worship is not easy for the preacher. So many things militate against the preparation for and worship of God.

THINGS THAT HINDER WORSHIP

A man who had the reputation of attending the worship services of his church always ahead of time was asked, "Why do you go to church early?" He replied, "It is a part of my religion not to disturb others when they worship." It could be that coming into the worship services ahead of time would add to the dignity and helpfulness of a worship service.

Some people talk to others in a worship service. This tends to hinder the worship of the persons near them. In worship services we are not to be spectators sitting on the side line. We are to be participants, showing some concern for the spiritual exercises that are under way. If we have our hearts set upon worship of God we are going to have concern for the entire services as we become a part of the various phases of worship. In some places people with small children allow them to disturb the worship. With nurseries provided this has been taken care of in most places. There is a danger that small children will be left in the nurseries when they should learn to worship along with their parents.

Wrong attitudes can hinder worship. We can hold a grudge, hate, dislike for a person or carry a "chip" on the shoulder and fail to enter into the spirit of worship. If one is wrong in his relationship to God he cannot worship. If you rebel against God when some misfortune befalls you, you cannot enter into a spirit of worship. In worship we have fellowship with God. In John's first epistle we find these words, "If we say that we have fellowship with him and walk in darkness, we lie and do not tell the truth:

But if we walk in the light as he is in the light, we have fellowship one with another, and the blood of Jesus Christ his Son cleanseth us from all sin." I John 1:6-7

Unconfessed and unforgiven sins will hinder our worship. This is true of any and of all would-be worshippers. Jesus taught that if we would be forgiven we must be willing to forgive men their trespasses. In the Model Prayer Jesus taught us to pray, "Forgive us our trespasses as we forgive those who trespass against us." We must come making confession of any and of all sin, with a willingness to forsake it, if we would feel and know the forgiving power of God in our hearts. We must have clean hands and a pure heart when we stand before God in the Holy place. No person can truly worship if he approves sin and wrong doing. If we regard iniquity then God will not hear and answer our prayers.

To be in a backslidden condition always breaks the fellowship between the soul and God. David had to confess and forsake sin before he could feel that he was in the good graces of God. The prodigal had to come to want, to himself, and to a confession before he could be restored to the fellowship of his father's home.

Disobedience to God hinders our worship. "Therefore him that knoweth to do good, and doeth it not, to him it is sin." James 4:17 If we love Jesus we will do what He says. Jesus asked, "Why do ye call me Lord, Lord and do not the things I say?" In worship we ask for divine blessings and we give God thanks for the granting of such. There is a great fact given in I John 3:22 which is as follows: "And whatsoever we ask, we receive of him, because we keep his commandments, and do those things that are pleasing in his sight."

If we are absorbed in other things, be they good or bad, we cannot enter into the spirit of worship. It is not always easy to bring our minds in from the things of the world and center them upon God and His greatness and goodness. Often people have some unpleasant things at home, in business, or in social life that make it very difficult to worship. Sports, pleasure, a fishing trip, or some other thing in which we have been engaged during the week makes it difficult to "be still and know that He is God". We must think His thoughts after Him if we are to be free and un-fettered in worship. Some great reverse in life or some successful deal in business may absorb our greatest concern in an entire worship service, so that we cannot enter into it fully and freely.

Pride, arrogance, haughtiness or some known or unknown idol may stand between us and God. These hinder in worship. Jesus said, "God is a spirit: and they that worship him must worship him in spirit and in truth." John 4:24 This is the kind of worshipper that God seeks and finds in fellowship with Him.

THE PURPOSE OF WORSHIP

Thus far we have considered the universal desire and need for worship. We have seen how necessary it is to prepare for worship. We thought of some things that hinder in and out of the regular worship services of the church. Now let us think of the purpose of worship. This is a good time to ask, "Why do I attend church? Do I attend church out of habit or because others go to church? Do I go to church to ease my sense of guilt before God? Do I go to church because I feel that the best people in my community attend church occasionally or regularly?"

In worship we honor and glorify God. "O come, let us worship, and bow down: let us kneel before the Lord our maker." Psalm 95:6 "Let everything that hath breath praise the Lord . . ." Psalm 150:6 "Let the words of my mouth, and the meditations of my heart be acceptable in thy sight, O Lord, my strength, and my redeemer." Psalm 19:14 This should be the highest desire and purpose of man. In true worship we discover and recognize the worth-ship of God. We pay tribute to Him for who He is and for what He does for us. In worship we recognize the true greatness, goodness, mercy, love, and long-suffering of God.

The purpose of worship is to have fellowship with God. He made us for this purpose. He redeemed us for this purpose. If we love God as we are commanded we will delight to meet Him in worship. We will delight to do His will. We sing, and many sing it from the heart:

"What a fellowship, what a joy divine,
Leaning on the everlasting arms;
What a blessedness, what a peace is mine,
Leaning on the everlasting arms."

In worship Christians are made stronger. If we continue to attend some church and are not getting better and growing stronger something is wrong either with you or the worship services in your church. The true worshipper gets a lift in worship. Feeding upon God's Word will give strength. So will having fellowship with other Christians. Often people say to the minister, "The service today was a real blessing to me." One faithful worshipper said to the minister, "The prayer today was just what I needed with my heart so heavily burdened." Another said, "As I sat in the congregation and thought, one of my great burdens was taken away and I could enter into the spirit of worship."

How refreshing it is to sing:

"Bless be the tie that binds our hearts in Christian love;
The fellowship of kindred minds is like to that above."

76

The purpose of worship is to receive information and inspiration. You will not get much out of worship if you are just an occasional visitor at church. You will not be made strong if you put little or nothing into worship. The minister as he leads the people in worship speaks to God in praise and prayer for the congregation. God speaks to us in and through the reading and the interpretation of His Word. God speaks to us through the preaching of His Word. It is true "That the entrance of thy word giveth light". As we worship we are encouraged to meet life's battles, duties, and responsibilities. True worship will have a washing and a cleansing effect upon those who worship. Life's burdens are made bearable and lighter. Comfort is found as we draw nigh to God.

In worship we are to create an atmosphere in which Christians are strengthened and concern and compassion for lost sinners is evident. It has been said, "When sinners come into our church services and they are not convicted of sin, then the church is convicted of sin." The three thousand people who professed faith in Christ and were baptized at Pentecost came out of a warm and compassionate atmosphere. Eggs are not hatched in refrigerators. Souls are born again in a spirit-filled and spirit-led atmosphere.

Let us ask again, "Why do we attend church? What is the purpose of maintaining costly and expensive church houses and programs?"

> "Some go to church for a walk,
> Some go there to laugh and talk,
> Some go there to see a friend,
> Some go there their time to spend,
> Some go there to gain a lover,
> Some go there their faults to cover,
> Some go there for illustration,
> Some go there for affectation,
> Some go there to doze and nod,
> Let me go there to worship God."   Author Unknown

SOME OF THE VITAL FACTORS
IN WORSHIP

There are many facets in worship. There are many designated places of worship. We must not overlook the fact that in every life there should be a trysting place. We should meet God in our quiet place or places. Every home should have a family altar. At the family altar the family should gather daily, if at all possible, to read some of the Scripture and to pray. In such an atmosphere every child should move, breathe, and have his being. The family altar will change things.

Music is important and vital in worship. Often I have been brought into a worshipful attitude as I have listened to the quiet music of the organ. Over and over again my soul has been filled and thrilled as I have been driving along the highway and tuned in on some great medley of hymns. We are to come into God's presence with singing. We are called to sing and make melody unto the Lord. Great congregational singing helps people to worship. It should be worshipful. Many have good voices with which to sing praises unto God. Choir numbers and other specials should be worshipful and Scriptural in message.

We are to make much of prayer in worship. We are to learn the secret of waiting before God. The Psalmist (40:1-3) says: "I waited patiently for the Lord, and he inclined unto me, and heard my cry. He brought me up also out of an horrible pit . . . And he hath put a new song in my mouth, even praise unto our God . . ." We are to take time to be holy. We are privileged to speak oft with our Lord.

In worship there should always be a prominent place for God's Word. It is to be given a large place in all of our church work. We are to give attention to what the Word says for us and to us in our generation. This should be done without altering it to fit our notions. Jesus said, "Search the

78

Scriptures; for in them ye think ye have eternal life: and they are they which testify of me." John 5:39. The Berean Christians searched the Word to see if the missionaries were telling it like the recorded Word. It is good to see people bringing their Bibles to church and opening them at the right time to hear the Word read.

Preaching the Word is a most vital part of worship. We are to preach the Word, not something else. There is no good substutite for the preaching of the Gospel. Paul was not ashamed of the Gospel. The Psalmist speaks of God magnifying his word above his name. God speaks to us through His recorded and revealed Word. It is authoritative. It is inspired. It does not change when all about us we see change and decay.

Martin Luther said, "People should never assemble without the preaching of the Word." In so many of the Protestant and Evangelical churches the pulpits are placed in the center of the church. Preaching the Word has been a most potent factor in our worship services. It should never be crowded out for anything else.

Giving is essential in worship. We are not to appear before God empty. We are urged to "bring an offering and come before the Lord". We are to do this upon the first day of the week. Every one of God's children are to bring an offering. It should be a proportionate gift. It is to be made in keeping with the ability of the giver. We should remember that it is God who giveth us power to get wealth. We cannot worship God as we ought when we are dishonest and stingy. God loves a cheerful giver. We are told in the Word that it is more blessed to give than to receive.

Every aspect and all phases of worship should be used, so that in our worship the purpose and plan of God for us shall be brought to fruition. The needs of people are involved in God's plan for us to worship. He can get along without any

79

one of us. However, we cannot get along without coming to Him in worship so that the deeper needs of the spiritual man can be met and realized.

CHAPTER NINE

A NEW HEART AND A NEW LIFE

"A new heart also will I give you, and a new Spirit will I put within you: and I will take away the stony heart out of your flesh, and I will give you an heart of flesh.

And I will put my Spirit within you, and cause you to walk in my statutes, and ye shall keep my judgments, and do them." Ezekiel 36:26-27

During the past days we have heard a great deal about human organ transplants. We have heard that a kidney was taken from one person and given to another. We have heard of several heart transplants, the first in South Africa. Since then several such operations have been performed. Things that "could not be done are being done". Modern day miracles are taking place in our midst. The prophet Ezekiel is talking about a "New Heart". This does not mean that some surgeon would cut out the heart of one person because it was bad and that another good heart would be given. He is talking of a strange but real change that would take place in the heart of a person who was sinful, and wrong in his relationship to God. It seems that the ancients thought of the heart as the seat of compassion. If one's heart was right then the acts and deeds of a person would be righteous and right.

A NEW HEART IS A NECESSITY

A new heart is a Divine necessity. This is true because man in his natural state is a sinner. He is a lost sinner. He is an alien before God. He is separated from God because of his sinful and unregenerate condition. The psalmist said, "I was shapen in iniquity, and in sin did my mother conceive me . . ." The prophet Isaiah says, "All we like sheep have gone astray, we have turned every one to his own way . . ." Paul says, "There is none good, no not one . . ." Again he says, "All have sinned and come short of the glory of God . . ." The prophet Jeremiah says, "The heart is deceitful and desperately wicked who can know it . . ." Before the flood God looked upon mankind and saw that the wickedness of man was great in the earth. Because of man's sins he destroyed all mankind, save one family.

Man in his natural and unregenerate state cannot find God. In 1 Corinthians 2:14 the Apostle says, "But the natural man receiveth not the things of the Spirit of God: for they are foolishness unto him; neither can he know them, because they are spiritually discerned."

Man cannot please God with the old heart. It must be made new. "Out of the heart are the issues of life. As a man thinketh in his heart, so is he." "Out of the heart proceed evil thoughts . . ." James tells us that no fountain can send forth both sweet and bitter water at the same time.

We know that without faith we cannot please God. The Bible states: "So then they that are in the flesh cannot please God . . . because the carnal mind is at enmity against God . . ." We are not to trust in our own heart but in God. We are to trust in God with all our heart. We are not to lean unto our own understanding. In Acts 8 the story is told of a man who thought that the power evident in the life of the Apostle could be bought. Peter rebuked him very sharply saying, "Thy money perish with thee, because thou hast thought that the gift of God may be purchased with money. Thou hast neither part nor lot in this matter: for thy heart is not right in the sight of God." Peter called on Simon to repent of this wickedness. He was urged to pray and ask God to forgive him of this sinful and evil thought. In the life of Pharaoh we see how deep in sin one can go when his heart is hardened against God and will not turn to God in obedience. The hearts of Annanias and Sapphira were sinful. Because of the sinful acts of mind and heart they felt that they could deceive God and others. Satan had filled the hearts of these two people. The seriousness of the sin was in the fact that they lied to God. They did this because their hearts were not right with God.

GOD PROMISES A NEW HEART

God assures man that he can have a New Heart. He assures man that he can have a New Spirit. This promise is not that man will have an improved nature, although he will have an improved nature, a changed attitude, and a new disposition to do right over against wrong. God is not promising man better living conditions, but man will live better and will help create a more wholesome environment in which to live. God's promise is plain — "A new Heart will I give you . . . a New Spirit will I put within you . . ." The old nature will be changed. The stony heart will be taken away and a new heart will be put in its place. The fulfillment of this promise assures man that the new heart is a Divine work. It is of God and not of man. "Therefore if any man be in Christ, he is a new creature: old things are passed away; behold all things are become new." 2 Corinthians 5:17. Paul says in Romans 8:9: "If any man have not the Spirit of Christ he is none of his." In other words, the Holy Spirit makes effective the work of Christ on the cross for our redemption. No man can have a changed heart without the work of the Holy Spirit.

THE NATURE OF THE CHANGE

We have thought about the necessity for a New Heart. We have also thought of the Promise God makes of a New Heart. In thinking of the change and the nature of it several simple things are involved. It seems to me that the heart Ezekiel is speaking about involves the same fundamental things that are dealt with in John 3 where Jesus and Nicodemus talk together. In other words the New Birth is involved in this transaction that assures one of a New Heart.

The work wrought in the life of the man with the old nature is a work of Grace. The change is mysterious. Jesus illustrates this by referring to the wind. The blowing of the wind is still a great mystery. So is the change wrought within a man when the Spirit of God regenerates him and makes him a new creature in Christ Jesus. Jesus said to Nicodemus, "Except a man be born again, he cannot see the kingdom of God." Again He says, "Except a man be born of water and of the Spirit, he cannot enter into the Kindgom of God." In the pronouncements of our Lord we find the supreme superlatives. The one great cardinal essential for one to be saved is — HE MUST BE BORN AGAIN. Not only is the change of the heart all of grace and mysterious but it is also SUPERNATURAL. God uses the Word to reveal man's need for a vital and living experience of Grace. His blood cleanses us from all sin. The Spirit effects the change. In this act which is supernatural there is a transformation. It is Regeneration and not education, or resolutions, or a resolve to do better. Such an act on the part of God is revolutionary. It is a New Life, with a New Master, with New motive power that moves us. It is a new life and not the turning over of a new leaf. In this transaction we also become partakers of a new nature. We are now under the mastery of a New Master.

84

When we have a new heart we become a member of God's family. God's work of grace is instantaneous. When done we can sing, "tis done, the great transaction's done, I am my Lord's, and He is mine."

TO HAVE THIS NEW HEART TWO STEPS MUST BE TAKEN

First the sinner must be convicted of his sins by the Holy Spirit. John 16:7-11 should be pondered. The Word of God is used to bring conviction. Over and over again the note of repentance is emphasized in the Bible. Unless sinners are willing to repent they cannot be saved. So often other things are emphasized as being essential. God commands people to repent. He does not command that which one cannot do. He calls us to repentance. He calls in so many different ways.

Unless the sinner repents of his sins he cannot be saved. Unless God brings him to repentance he cannot come to repentance. Many of the great prophets of the Old Testament emphasized the importance of repentance before God could look with favor upon a nation or a person. God's people were called upon to repent. This idea is couched in a well known passage, 2 Chronicles 7:14: "If my people, which are called by name, shall humble themselves, and pray, and seek my face, and turn from their wicked ways; then will I hear from heaven, and will forgive their sin, and will heal their land." Isaiah entreats: "Let the wicked forsake his way, and the unrighteous man his thoughts: and let him return unto our Lord, for he will have mercy upon him: and to our God, for he will abundantly pardon." Isaiah 55:7

In Ezekiel the prophet gives an illustration of the potter at the potter's wheel. The potter took a vessel of clay that was marred in the making and he made it over again. "So he made it again, another vessel as seemed good to the potter to make it." When Jesus touched the man born blind, as

85

recorded in John 9, he was never the same man again. He did not understand the miracle. However, he did say, "One thing I know, that, whereas I was blind, now I see."

Faith is the second step one must take. It is repentance toward God and faith in our Lord Jesus Christ. Faith means that we take God at His word. It is really the substance of things hoped for, the evidence of things not seen. When the Philippian jailer asked, "Sirs, what must I do to be saved?", they said, "Believe on the Lord Jesus Christ. and thou shalt be saved." Acts 16:30-31

When people on the day of Pentecost were under conviction they cried out, "Men and brethren what must we do?" Peter replied, "Repent, and be baptized every one of you in the name of Jesus Christ for the remission of sins, and ye shall receive the gift of the Holy Spirit." There could not have been any genuine repentance without faith in Jesus Christ as Savior and Lord.

When the Ethiopian had placed his faith in Jesus as his Savior he was ready to follow the example of Jesus in New Testament baptism. Jesus came into the world to save sinners. He plainly states that faith (trust or belief) brings salvation to the believer. In John 5:24 He says, "Verily, verily I say unto you, he that heareth my word, and believeth on him that sent me hath everlasting life, and shall not come into condemnation; but is passed from death unto life." The words in this Scripture are found in John 3:14-19 and in John 3:36.

When one experiences a change in his own heart and life he will know it. He will be able to tell others about this experience. He will be able to sing, "What a wonderful change in my life has been wrought since Jesus came into my heart." Let us claim the great and gracious promise in our text of Scripture. "A new heart also I will give you, and a new spirit will I put within you; and I will take away the stony heart out of your flesh, and I will give you an heart of flesh. And I will put my spirit within you, and cause you to walk in my statues, and ye shall keep my judgements, and do them."

CHAPTER TEN

MAKING WISE AND SAFE INVESTMENTS

"What? Know ye not that your body is the temple of the Holy Spirit which is in you, which ye have of God, and ye are not your own? For ye are bought with a price: therefore glorify God in your body, and in your spirit, which are God's." 1 Corinthians 6:19-20.

If God is our creator and the sustainer of life then we are under obligation to honor God by the wise and the right use of life. Life is a trust and should be handled as such. Since God has made such investments in us, we should make wise investments for Him. We have been created and recreated for high and worthy ends. No man can understand life. It has been said, "The chief end of man is to serve God and to glorify Him." During the days of the depression in the early thirties when so many large businesses were failing, one large company among others weathered the storm. The head of this concern said, "We have tried to safe-guard the principal. We have not been too concerned about quick salability nor large dividends." This man was concerned with safe-guarding that which had been entrusted to him. He was satisfied with a reasonable return from the money invested. All who have been entrusted with life should so use it that when the accounting day comes, as it will, we can give a good account of our stewardship.

WE SHOULD INVEST LIFE WHERE IT WILL COUNT FOR THE MOST

We have no right to defile life. In our habits we should see that such will make for the building of Christian character. We are to keep ourselves pure. Paul says we are to think upon things that are true, honest, just, pure, lovely, and of good report. Then he adds, "If there be any virtue, and if there be any praise, think on these things." Philippians 4:8 An astronomer was looking into his telescope and as he was beholding the wonders of God in the heavens he said, "I am thinking thy thoughts after thee, O God."

We have no right to dissipate or waste life. It is sad to see a young man or a young woman with strong and attractive bodies who waste them upon the desert air. How many spend all in riotous living! The person who defiles his body will be destroyed. We should take the long look and determine early in life that we will let God have His way in our lives.

We have no right to divide life. It seems that many try to serve two masters. Jesus said, "No man can serve two masters: for either he will hate the one, and love the other; or else he will hold to the one and despise the other. Ye cannot serve God and mammon." Matthew 6:24 In Romans 12:1-2 Paul enjoins us to present our bodies as a living sacrifice unto God. A young woman speaking at a Student Volunteer meeting during my college days said in her devotional message, "As a Christian and a volunteer for mission service I must be willing to give Jesus the keys to every room in my life. This I have tried to do and would like to continue doing this in His service." This indeed is a good picture of complete dedication and surrender to Christ. Every Christian should be willing to consecrate his service daily to the Lord.

God expects not the leftovers but the best. This is to be expected. We sing, "Take my life and let it be consecrated, Lord, to thee." We also sing in many of our churches,

"Give of your best to the master:
Give of the strength of your youth;
Clad in salvation's full armor,
Join in the battle for truth."

THE INVESTMENT OF INFLUENCE

I cannot define influence. However, it is a tremendous power in the life of an individual. It is often bad. It is also godly and transforming. Many influences go into the making of a great character. Your parents, teachers, friends, and pastors have had some part in making you what you are now. Like the warm rays of the sunshine the rays of Christian influence have fallen upon your life. Our influences are radio-active. Throw a stone into a lake and watch the concentric waves as they move toward the shore. Lift your arms and you disturb all the atmosphere about you. The ocean would be a dead calm if it were not for the influence of the sun, moon, and the wind. Jesus was talking about influence when he said, "Ye are the light of the world . . . Ye are the salt of the earth." These two forces are tremendous. What a power for good is a Christian fully committed to God. Such persons do not fit into the mold of the world.

There are people who have a Godly influence while there are those who live ungodly and unholy lives and pull others along their sinful ways. Men like Nero, Alexander, Herod, Darrow, Ingersol, Stalin, Hitler, and others still live through their wicked influences. Many Christians who are never in the limelight live on in and through those whom they have influenced to put their trust in Christ and to live for Him who died for them. A young man said of his sweetheart, "I would give the world if I could be as good, and at the same

time be as happy as you." Godly people can influence the
ungodly. They can also have a wholesome and an helpful
influence upon their fellow Christians. We are to so live that
we will encourage others by our example to live dedicated
and committed lives. There are too many church people who
live lives that are not in keeping with their profession.

A WISE INVESTMENT OF TIME

"See then that ye walk circumspectly, not as fools, but as
wise, redeeming the time, because the days are evil."
Ephesians 5:15-16 We do not make time. It is a gift from
God. It is a trust. Walking circumspectly and using time so as
to bless and help others is our privilege and our
responsibility.

"Time is: Too slow for those who wait
Too swift for those who fear,
Too long for those who suffer,
Too short for those who rejoice,
But for those who love, time is not."

Henry Van Dyke

Think of how God uses time. In six days He made all
things. On the seventh day He rested. God is busy daily doing
things for us. Jesus is at the right hand of God making
intercession on our behalf. God expects us to use time wisely
and well. In the right use of time we can bless and help. In
the wrong use of time we can curse, and blight the lives of
others. Benjamin Franklin said: "Dost thou love life? Then
do not squander time, for this is the stuff that life is made
of."

A common excuse offered for not doing some things that
we should do is, "I do not have the time." Sometimes we do
not have time to do the things that need to be done because
we waste time, or we spend it on some things that should be
left undone. We all have the same number of hours to do

90

things that should claim our attention.

"Time worketh, let me work too
Time undoeth, let me do,
As busy as time my work I'd ply,
'Til I rest the rest of eternity."

Time should not be spent in idleness. It has been said, "Idleness is the sepulchre of the dreamer."

Another said, "The idle brain is the devil's workshop." It is not easy to use time wisely and helpfully. Many people waste time in various ways. Time is too precious to waste it on filthy reading, degrading shows, and sinful amusements.

There are many ways whereby we can invest time wisely. We can read good books, study the Bible for enrichment and enlightment, worship God faithfully and cultivate the friendship of the right kind of people. We can find some outlet in service to our fellowman, learn to do well the work to which we have devoted our lives, practice daily the presence of Jesus, and seek to live by the principles set forth in the New Testament for the Christian. Paul could say, "Christ shall be magnified in my life whether by life or by death . . ." and also "For me to live is Christ, to die is gain."

"I love in solitude to shed the penitential tear,
And all his promises to plead where none but God can hear."

If we would attain the heights in life we must make the right use of time. The poet says:

"The heights of great men reached and kept
Were not attained by sudden flight,
But they, while their companions slept,
Were toiling upward in the night."

THE INVESTMENT OF TALENT

Every person has some latent power or talent that can be used. In the parable of the talents they were given out, it is said, "To every man according to his several ability . . ." Matthew 25:15 In other words each man's ability was taken into consideration. The man with five talents doubled them by the accounting time. The man with two also doubled his and he, too, heard, "Well done, thou good and faithful servant; thou hast been faithful over a few things, I will make thee ruler over many things: enter thou into the joy of thy Lord." Matthew 24:23. The man who received one talent failed to use it. He hid it in the ground and brought condemnation upon himself because he failed to use the one talent. Moses had a rod which was blessed of God. A small boy had a lunch which when given to Jesus was blessed of Him and used to feed a great crowd. On one occasion Jenny Lynn was asked how she could sing so sweetly, and she replied, "I sing for the ear of God." Florence Nightingale, the angel of mercy in the Crimean war said, "I let Christ have all there is in me." To invest wisely and well our talents will mean:

"Heads through which Christ may think;
Hands through which Christ may serve;
Hearts through which Christ may love;
Voices through which Christ may sing, teach, and
preach."

THE INVESTMENT OF MATERIAL THINGS

This is perhaps the one thing about which most people are concerned. People who are frugal and thrifty save a little for the day when it will be needed. Much is said in the Bible about money. Jesus also had a great deal to say about material things, and the right acquisition of them, and the wise use of wealth. He emphasizes the importance of laying up treasures in heaven. The Bible enjoins people to lay aside material substance to be used in Kingdom work. Read Malachi 3:8-10, Leviticus 27:30, Deuteronomy 8:18,

Deuteronomy 16 and 17, Proverbs 3:9, Matthew 6:19-31, 2 Corinthians 8:7-9, 2 Corinthians 8:5, 1 Corinthians 9:13-18, and 1 Timothy 6:17-19.

There are many ways and places in which we can invest material things. The care of the work of the local church calls for money. Home missions, State Missions, and Foreign Missions demand liberal support on the part of Christians. We are commanded to go unto the uttermost part of the earth. Acts 1:8 and Matthew 28:18-20. We are to give liberally of that which has been entrusted to us. To be good and faithful stewards of our possessions is a high and a holy privilege. God's Kingdom business is the biggest business in the world. Every person should give on every Lord's day a liberal gift, as he has been prospered, and as he is able for the support of the entire program of the Kingdom. God's program is inclusive of teaching, preaching, and healing. In our benevolent institutions we take care of the sick, and aged, and the orphan children. In this program we also help train young people in our colleges and in our seminaries. We undergird all of the missionaries at home and abroad. This means transportation, food, clothes, lodging, and enough money to take care of other normal needs in their family life. There are some investments we can make in God's work that will bear fruit and bring results after we go home to our heavenly reward. One good way to lose material things is to hold them and save them selfishly. One way to save material things is to lay up treasure in heaven. We can make eternal investments as we bring the tithes and the offerings into God's storehouse for His work. Surely, it is more blessed to give than it is to receive. The Scripture says, "The liberal soul shall grow fat", and "The Lord loveth a cheerful giver". Just keep on giving until God stops giving to you. Dr. George W. Truett said, "A Christian man, wrong on the matter of money, is likely to be more seriously wrong on every other question in religion." A stingy Christian cannot be the best kind of Christian.

John Ruskin said that he had attended church for 30 years and had heard over 1500 sermons but had never heard a sermon on "The Struggle Between Mammon and God". Surely in our day and generation in almost all congregations sermons are preached dealing with money and man's relationship to it.

THE INVESTMENT OF INTELLIGENCE

Jesus sums up the law and the prophets by saying, "Thou shalt love the Lord thy God with all thy heart, and with all thy soul, and with all thy mind, and with all thy strength: this is the first commandment. And the second is like unto this, namely, thou shalt love thy neighbor as thyself. There is none other commandment greater than these." Mark 12:30, 31. When Jesus makes these two statements He includes the whole man. The whole potential powers of man are wrapped up in these vital words. Our power to reason, will, think, and study distinguishes us from lower animals. Thoughts survive death. Many wonderful thoughts are preserved for us in writings. Pascal said, "The good thought is greater than all the material universe." Worthy and worthwhile endeavors come as a result of intelligent thinking. The Psalmist said, "I thought on my ways, and turned my feet unto thy testimonies." Psalm 119:59 In James 1:5 are these words, "If any man lack wisdom let him ask of God . . ." In 2 Timothy 2:15 are these words, "Study to show thyself approved unto God, a workman that needeth not be ashamed, rightly dividing the word of truth." We should develop our minds to the very best of our ability and use our intelligence to serve God and our fellowman. Intelligence is the capacity for higher forms of knowledge and superior action. When human intelligence is divorced from Christ then it goes astray. It is tragic to see a person with a keen mind, highly trained and educated, who uses it in a degrading and destructive manner.

One of the great scientists, George Washington Carver, came out of obscurity to fame and honor. He gave God the credit, honor and glory for his ability to create. Many poets, artists, musicians, and writers have blessed us with their works. We are the better because their lives touched ours.

There are so many ways in which we can enrich our minds. Wordsworth used to sit for hours by a brook or under the shade of a tree observing the flowers or listening to the voice of a bird. So he wrote:

"Whose dwelling is the light of setting suns,
And the round ocean and the living air,
And the blue sky, and in the heart of man."

If we listen to the voice of God, we, too, will hear Him speaking to us. God spoke to Elijah under the juniper tree. He spoke to John the Baptist in the wilderness. He spoke to Paul while he was in Arabia. He communed with Jesus by the sea of Galilee. God spoke to Moses out of the burning bush. We can hear that still small voice if we will be still and listen for it.

Ben Franklin said on one occasion, "If a man empties his purse into his head no one can take it away from him." A father with limited educational advantages and opportunities said to his son with many advantages beyond those of his father, "Son, more will be expected of you because you are having far greater advantages than I had." William Carey and Alexander Duff with their keen minds and a multiplicity of talents labored in India for some years. Duff stated a truth when he said, "My chief objective is in setting up an institution where Hindu youth can be instructed in the principles of the Christian religion. If you give the people knowledge without religion, rest assured that it would be the greatest blunder politically that ever was made." In that school the Bible was the chief book. What will happen to a nation that gives attention to the mind but leaves out the great guiding principles of morality and Christian living? There have been many suicides in Japan among the brilliant students of the Imperial University of Japan. Why has this been true? They had no anchor for the soul. In what they had learned there was no assurance of the beyond. They had become atheistic and fatalistic.

> "Let knowledge grow from more to more,
> But more of reverence in us dwell,
> That both mind and soul according well,
> May make one music as before,
> But vaster."

By: Tennyson

CHAPTER ELEVEN

ASSURANCE IN SALVATION
(Read Matthew 7:15-23)

There are many passages of Scripture which assure the Christian that he has salvation. This he can know and others also should feel confident that his profession of salvation in Christ is real. Such passages as John 3:14-21, 36, and John 5:24 have in them the note of certainty. This is pointed up in Ephesians 2:8-10, Acts 16:31, and Acts 4:12. In Titus 2:11-14 we find the note of assurance stated. The Apostle Paul sounded the note of certainty in 1 Timothy 1:15 and in 2 Timothy 1:12.

Many of our great hymns stress the note of assurance. One of the popular hymn writers, though physically blind, and yet with clear spiritual sight, could write one of the great hymns sung by millions of people who found salvation in Christ. Think of these wonderful words:

"Blessed assurance, Jesus is mine!
Oh, what a foretaste of glory divine!
Heir of salvation, purchase of God,
Born of His Spirit, washed in His blood.
Perfect submission, perfect delight,
Visions of rapture now burst on my sight;
Angels descending, bring from above

97

Echoes of mercy, whispers of love.
Perfect submission, all is at rest,
I in my Savior am happy and blest;
Watching and waiting, looking above,
Filled with His goodness, lost in His love.

Chorus:
This is my story, this is my song,
Praising my Savior, all the day long;
This is my story, this is my song,
Praising my Savior all the day long."

A young woman had a dream. In that dream she was condemned to die. However, she was told that if she could find someone who would testify that she was a Christian she would not be put to death. The only persons that could say she was a Christian were those who said that she had professed to be a Christian. She awoke from that dream with a desire to dedicate her life to God and tell by her daily living that she truly was a New Creation in Christ Jesus.

ARE YOU SAVED?

There are some simple questions each person should ask himself. Most of us have filled out questionnaires. Simple questions are asked as to age, race, background, etc. We answer these positively but there is too much uncertainty among people concerning the most important fact of life. When asked, Are you a Christian? many reply by saying, "I am a member of the church," or "I hope I am", or "I am trying to be", or "I can't be sure". Some years ago I walked into the office of the power and light company in my city to pay my electric bill. Several people in there were engaged in an argument. One spoke up and said, "Here is the preacher, ask him the question." A young woman who worked in the office had just stated that she had never seen a Christian. She had the idea that no person could know until he reached the

98

end of life's journey that he was or was not saved. She held to some great Bible truths but was interpreting them out of context. My reply to the question, "Have you ever seen a Christian?" was simple and direct. "Yes, I have seen many people who had trusted Christ as Savior and Lord, and were by virtue of this fact a Born Again Christian." Then I said, "I am a Christian but not as good as I want to be and hope to be."

Some people think you are saved by keeping the Sermon on the Mount. Others say you are saved by keeping the Golden Rule. Still others say that if you make a passing grade on the ten commandments you are a Christian. There are some people who say, "If you do the best you can you are saved." Who does the best he can?

Paul knew that Jesus came to save sinners. He knew that he as the chief of sinners had been saved by the one who came for this purpose. You cannot afford to be wrong on this important matter.

HOW CAN YOU KNOW THAT YOU ARE SAVED?

Look at the evidence. You can know that you are a saved sinner because you were there when this great transaction took place. You realized that Jesus died on the cross for sinners. Out of conviction for sins you accepted what Jesus did on the cross for you. You accepted His sacrifice as payment in full for your sin debt. That was indeed a happy day.

Many of the great hymn writers have helped us to sing about the new life in Christ. How could you sing "Blessed Assurance" and "My Hope is Built on Nothing Less Than Jesus Blood and Righteousness" if there were any doubt about your salvation? The blind man who was touched by Jesus knew that whereas he had been blind now he could see.

He also knew that he was at one time lost but now he was found. Jesus did it all.

Your profession of faith in Christ tells of a change in your life. You made a confession of sin and were willing to turn from sin to Jesus for salvation. This you did, if your profession were real. Paul in Romans 10:9-10 says, "If thou shalt confess with thy mouth the Lord Jesus, and shalt believe in thine heart that God hath raised him from the dead, thou shalt be saved. For with the heart man believeth unto righteousness; and with the mouth confession is made unto salvation." Jesus says, "Whosoever therefore shall confess me before men, him will I also confess before my Father which is in Heaven." Matthew 10:32-33.

Your attitudes following your confession and baptism will have something to say. Your attitude toward sin will be very revealing. Your attitude toward God, His church, and His people will also be revealed in you. Time and time again we see men and women who turned from a life of sin to salvation in Christ. We can tell that a wonderful change in their habits, attitudes and interest has taken place. Among all the cures that people try when in sin none are as far reaching and lasting as that which comes when they really turn from sin to Jesus for cleansing and for forgiveness.

When we are saved we love the brethren. Jesus said, "By this shall all men know that ye are my disciples, that you have love one for another." Again we read what John said, "We know that we have passed from death unto life because we love the brethren . . . If any man say I love God and hate his brother, he is a liar." How can professed Christian men and women hate each other? What is the result of a church with members in it who will not even be Christ-like in his or her attitude toward another brother or sister? When this is true the church loses her influence with men and women who need to be reached with the Gospel.

The Holy Spirit bears witness with our spirit that we are God's children. He alone can seal us. We may be mistaken about a person who says, "I am a Christian." The Holy Spirit cannot and will not be mistaken. We need to ponder the truth — "The Spirit himself beareth witness with our spirit that we are children of God . . ." and "For as many as are led by the Spirit they are the children of God" and "If any man have not the Spirit of Christ he is none of his."

We know that we have been saved because we have compassion and concern for others. Was this not true when you first met the Lord and were saved? Did you not turn in your thought to a brother, sister, or friend? Did you not try to witness to him or to her? It is perfectly natural and normal for a Christian to desire the salvation of another sinner. When Jesus looked upon the multitudes he was moved with compassion and with outstretched hands. Andrew went after his brother Peter. Philip went after Nathaniel. Paul's heart's desire and prayer to God for his people was that they be saved. When the man of Gadara met Jesus and was saved he wanted to go with Jesus. However, Jesus commanded that he go to his friends and to his own people.

HOW CAN OTHER PEOPLE KNOW THAT YOU ARE A CHRISTIAN?

All that we have said previously will be very convincing if we are true in our practice of these things which we have professed to believe. Hypocrisy is very easily detected. It is not easy to cover up.

We are going to be known by our fruits, deeds, acts, words, and life. One of the most convincing evidences of the Gospel is a person who lives the Christian life. Jesus said, "By their fruits ye shall know them . . . a good tree bringeth forth good fruit but an evil tree bringeth forth evil fruit . . ." John the Baptist urged the people to "Bring forth fruit meet for repentance . . ." There is nothing so convincing among people as the life of a person who has been bound down by sinful habits, who comes to know Jesus as his Savior and makes this known publicly and goes out to walk in a new way and to live a transformed life. People will take note of this. Over and over again men have been brought out of darkness into light, out of bondage into the freedom that is in Christ.

A wicked man was brought into a vital relationship with Jesus as his personal Savior and Lord. The men who worked for him knew that he was sinful and used God's name in vain rather freely. They wondered how he would behave on the job when things did not go so well. Now this new Christian was really on trial. When something went wrong that had previously caused him to use profanity his attitude and speech were different now. One of the men said to a fellow worker, "He's got it." He had had an experience that changed his life completely. This others could see and feel.

CHAPTER TWELVE

JESUS CALLS US

"And Jesus, walking by the sea of Galilee, saw two brethren, Simon called Peter, and Andrew his brother, casting a net into the sea: for they were fishers. And he said unto them, Follow me, and I will make you fishers of men.

And they straightway left their nets, and followed him."

Matthew 4:18-20

It is interesting to note how God calls people. He calls through His Word. He calls through his Holy Spirit. He calls through ministers and missionaries. He calls through the plain humble everyday Christian. God often speaks to us through our consciences and better judgment.

There are many hymns that we sing which carry out the theme of this sermon. When the sermon has been delivered and the invitation is sung we find the idea of the call enunciated. How many times have we heard, "Softly and tenderly Jesus is calling, calling for you"! Mr. B. B. McKinney in one of his great hymns expresses this idea when he says, "Take up thy cross and follow me, I heard the Master say"!

Mrs. Cecil F. Alexander has written a great hymn entitled "Jesus Calls Us".

"Jesus calls us; o'er the tumult of our life's wild,

103

restless sea,
Day by day His sweet voice soundeth, saying,
Christian follow me."

There are many examples in the Scriptures where God calls people to come and follow Christ. As a matter of fact the call of Jesus is to the individual to come confessing his sins, forsaking them, and professing openly his faith in Christ as his Savior and Lord.

We know from experience that the call of Jesus is very real and that when we hear His call and obey Him, life is transformed. The four fishermen who saw Jesus and heard Him that day obeyed Him immediately, left the fishing business and followed Him.

JESUS CALLS TO DISCIPLESHIP

In the above scripture passage is seen Jesus' call to Andrew and Peter. He also said to James and to John, "Follow me and I will make you fishers of men." There was prompt obedience in each case. There was no delay. The call of Jesus deserves prompt and immediate obedience. Too much is involved to defer, neglect, or delay a right and a reasonable response to His call. This call involves life or death. It involves heaven or hell. It is a call from darkness to light.

JESUS CALLS ALL TYPES OF PEOPLE

The call of Christ is most inclusive. It is interesting to observe how Abraham, Moses, Jeremiah, and Isaiah were called, each in a different way. He called the rich young ruler who was so near to eternal life and yet so far away. Things stood between him and the call of the Master of men to a higher and a more lasting way. He called to Nicodemus the learned Rabbi who became His disciple. He called to Governor Pilate who saw no fault in Him, yet yielded to the

104

cry of the rabble who were bent on crucifying Jesus. He called to King Agrippa and King Herod. He called to the scarlet woman whose sins were forgiven. God the Father, God the Son, and God the Holy Spirit call the rich and the poor, the high and the low, and the learned and the unlearned. Each is called to deny self and take up "his cross" and follow Christ. Aren't you glad that God says in His Word, "For whosoever will, let him take the water of life freely"? Then, too, He says "For whosoever shall call upon the name of the Lord shall be saved." Romans 10:13

THE CALLS THAT COME TO US
FROM DIFFERENT DIRECTIONS

Did you ever hear your mother calling you and at the same time your father calling from some other direction? Did you ever hear some one passing by calling you? There is never any conflict in the calls that come to us from the Triune God. It is interesting to read in Isaiah 6 how God called from above to young Isaiah. He heard the call and responded to this plea and call from the heart of God. Paul also heard the voice coming from above.

There are calls that come from within. This is often the voice of God or of Conscience, or both. These should be heeded. Then there are calls that come from without. As we look upon the world today with its war, hunger, disease, and suffering what person among us can fail to hear and to see the need of the world? We are to look upon the harvest that is truly great. We are to consider the need for laborers in this needy and suffering world. When Jesus looked upon the crowds that stood in need He had compassion upon them.

JESUS CALLS US TO WITNESS
AND TO WIN

You were called to salvation and were saved to tell others

about the Savior. When you were saved, if you were, the good news was on its way to another. All Christians are commanded to go tell others. Matthew 28:18-20 and Acts 1:8. Just as John was a man sent from God to "bear witness of that light", so are we. This is indeed a day of good tidings and we should not keep silent about it.

Jesus called fishermen to be his disciples. They were commissioned and commanded to go and make other disciples. We were not saved and commanded to sit by and let the rest of the world go to hell. In Proverbs we find a commanding statement: "The fruit of the righteous is a tree of life; and he that winneth souls is wise." Proverbs 11:30. In Daniel 12:3 we find a most significant statement: "And they that be wise shall shine as the brightness of the firmament; and they that turn many to righteousness as the stars forever and ever." Every Christian should be employed in the King's business on a full time basis. There are some very graphic words in the New Testament that show the Christian "Going", "Making", "Baptizing", and "Teaching". This is involved in the Christian's commission. Matthew 28:18-20

JESUS CALLS US TO VISIT
WITH A PURPOSE

Too many visits made by church people are pointless and purposeless. When one visits to carry idle tales, useless gossip, and hurtful hearsay, he is not only wasting time but hurting those who are involved. We need to ask when we hear some tale about a person, "Is this thing so? Is it kind? Would it do any good to tell it?" We need to heed what the Psalmist has to say in Psalm 39:1: "I said, I will take heed to my ways, that I sin not with my tongue: I will keep my mouth with a bridle, while the wicked is before me." When some people come into the sick room they are like rays of sunshine. Their visit does more good than the medicine. Others make us feel like we need a bath.

I had just visited a member of the church where I was pastor. The patient seemed to be cheered and helped by my visit. About the time I was in the act of leaving one of my elderly members came in and greeted the patient cordially and then said, "Well, Mae, I never saw you looking so bad." She set the patient back without a planned intention of so doing. Our visits should be with a desire to help the person we visit whether that person be sick or well, lost or saved. James tells us, "Pure religion and undefiled before God and the Father is this: To visit the fatherless and widows in their affliction, and to keep himself unspotted from the world." Jesus says we visit Him when we visit them that He loves and cares for when He says "Inasmuch as ye did it unto one of the least of these, my brethren, ye did it unto me." Matthew 25:40 Let us not forget that God visited us. Jesus came to visit among men, and to minister unto them. The Holy Spirit was promised and He came to be with us, to visit with us, until Jesus comes again.

The story is told of a very active layman who told his pastor that he could count on him to do most anything except to visit. He said, "Pastor I am not cut out for that kind of work." One night the pastor called this layman to come and take him to the hospital to see a mutual friend who was very ill. The pastor's car was out of commission. The sick man was lost and needed the Savior. In a brief visit the pastor presented the plan of salvation and called on his lay brother to pray. The sick man was saved. On the way home the layman said to his pastor, "Pastor, it was hard to get me started, but I dare anyone to stop me now."

JESUS CALLS US TO CONSECRATION AND FULL SURRENDER

The record says about the first disciples of Jesus, "They

107

forsook all and followed Him." When you became a disciple of Jesus did you make a full surrender to Him? Were you then and are you now making a complete committal of all to Christ? Have you consecrated all to Jesus? It is much easier to sing, "Take my life and let it be consecrated Lord to thee . . ." than it is to do what we sing. So often I have tried to sing, "I surrender all, all to thee my blessed Savior . . ." but could not sing it in the full meaning of the words. We need to read again and again Romans 12:1-2 and Romans 6:11-13. One week in various places in religious meetings all the persons bringing the devotional messages read Romans 12:1-2. The thought came to me, "Do we just read Romans 12:1-2 without realizing that when we are "wholly" committed to Christ this is true and genuine consecration? In true surrender and consecration God gets all of us and the best comes to us.

JESUS CALLS US TO PRAY

This is a personal call. It means to be submissive to His will. It means that we are to pray believingly. Jesus said, "But thou, when thou prayest, enter into thy closet . . . pray to thy Father which is in secret." He also said, "And when thou prayest, thou shalt not be as the hypocrites are: for they love to pray standing in the synagogues and in the corners of the streets, that they may be seen of men." Matthew 6:5.

The prayer of the Pharisee shows how one can be a hypocrite in his prayer life. The Publican prayed, "God be merciful to me a sinner." This is the man who went down to his house justified. The faithful saints were all together in one place praying when the power of the Holy Spirit came upon them on the day of Pentecost. In 2 Chronicles 7:14 people were called to humble themselves, pray, and seek God's face, and turn from their wicked ways, then God assures them that he will hear from heaven, will forgive their sins, and heal their land. The writer of Hebrews enjoins us to "Come boldly unto

108

the throne of grace, that we may obtain mercy, and find grace to help in time of need." Paul tells us that the effectual, fervent prayer of a righteous man availeth much. In Acts 12 we find the church in prayer. The people literally prayed Peter out of jail. We are reminded in Matthew 18 that where two or three are together Christ is there. We are also assured that if any two shall agree on any one thing it shall be done for them.

PRAYER GETS RESULTS

A young man wanted to win his father to Christ. He asked three friends to join with him in an effort to win him. The son prepared the way by asking his father if it would be acceptable for these three friends to come and join him in this effort. When the friends arrived the son said, "Dad, I want you to be a Christian. I have asked these three friends to come so we can talk and pray with you." After talking and praying the father put his arm around his son and said, "Mark, I am so glad you came. This is the best thing you have ever done for me." In this brief visit with those who cared and were concerned enough to do something about it, a lost father was brought to know Christ as Savior and Lord. "And he said unto them, follow me and I will make you fishers of men."

CHAPTER THIRTEEN

THE WORK OF THE HOLY SPIRIT

Jesus said, "Behold I send the promise of my Father upon you: but tarry ye in the city of Jerusalem, until ye be endued with power from on high." Luke 24:49. Again Jesus said, "And I will pray the Father, and he shall give you another Comforter, that he may abide with you forever . . . I will not leave you comfortless: I will come to you." John 14:16-18. This promise was fulfilled on the day of Pentecost when the church was assembled waiting for the fulfillment of this promise made by Jesus. Acts 2 gives us a vivid picture of what happened when the Spirit of God came upon His people. They were assured that they would have power after that the Holy Spirit would come upon them. Then they would have power to be witnesses unto the ends of the earth. Acts 1:8.

There are 110 references in the Old Testament to the Holy Spirit. In the New Testament there are 269 references to the Holy Spirit and His work. Too many people are ignorant of the work of the Holy Spirit. We cannot know and understand the truth of the Bible without His illuminating and guiding presence. Jesus said, When he, the Spirit of Truth, is come, He will guide you into all truth . . . and will shew you things to come." John 16:13

Let us consider some of the areas in which the Holy Spirit works.

THE WORK OF THE HOLY SPIRIT
IN REGENERATION

He uses the Word of God to bring conviction for sin. Jesus told Nicodemus that he needed to be born again. He needed to be convicted of sin. He needed to be converted from sin. He told this Rabbi that unless he were born of the Spirit he could not see the Kingdom of God. Again he said, "Except a man be born of water and of the Spirit, he cannot enter into the Kingdom of God." John 3:5. Jesus said just before he went back to the Father, "And when he is come, he will reprove the world of sin, and of righteousness, and of judgment: of sin, because they believe not on me; of righteousness, because I go to my Father, and ye see me no more; of judgment, because the prince of this world is judged." John 16:8-11.

The Holy Spirit makes the Word effective in the hearer's heart. He "pricks", "quickens", and "cleanses" the heart. We need to set again and again in our minds and hearts Hebrews 4:12: "For the Word of God is quick, and powerful, and sharper than any two edged sword, piercing even to the dividing asunder of soul and spirit, and of the joints and marrow, and is a discerner of the thoughts and intents of the heart."

There can be no salvation from sin without the work of the Holy Spirit who alone makes effective the work Christ has done on the cross for the redemption of the sinner. There are people who deny the deity of Jesus and who claim to be Christian. How can this be? There are people who say they believe in God the Father and in Christ but do not believe in the Holy Spirit. How can such a person become a Christian? The Holy Spirit brings conviction, contrition, and conversion to the sinner. Too often those of us who seek to win sinners feel that we have failed. Let us remember that it is the Holy Spirit who will bring the sinner to faith and repentance and not we. Paul found certain disciples at Ephesus who had been baptized but who had not even heard that there was such a person as the Holy Spirit. Something then took place among these baptized "believers" that had not been previously experienced.

THE HOLY SPIRIT BEARS WITNESS
WITH OUR SPIRIT

He not only brings regeneration but He assures us that we have been saved. Can we be assured of salvation here and now? We sing:

"Blessed assurance, Jesus is mine!
Oh what a foretaste of glory divine!
Heir of salvation, purchase of God,
Born of His Spirit, washed in His blood.
This is my story, this is my song,
Praising my Savior all the day long;
This is my story, this is my song,
Praising my Savior all the day long."

Fanny J. Crosby

Catherine Booth said that we should not tell any person that he is saved. This is the business of the Holy Spirit. If any person does not have the Holy Spirit he does not belong to Christ. "The Spirit himself beareth witness with our spirit, that we are the children of God." Romans 8:16. Again the apostle Paul says, "For as many as are led by the Spirit of God, they are the children of God." Romans 8:14. In Ephesians 4:30 we find these significant words, "And grieve not the Holy Spirit of God, whereby ye are sealed unto the day of redemption."

Because of what God has done in Christ and through the

113

work of His Spirit the Christian can sing, "Oh happy day, that fixed my choice on thee, my Savior and my God . . ." Because of Paul's experience with Jesus Christ he could say with all assurance and hope, "This is a faithful saying, and worthy of all acceptation, that Christ Jesus came into the world to save sinners; of whom I am chief." 1 Timothy 1:15.

THE HOLY SPIRIT HONORS CHRIST

The Holy Spirit honors the Word. He inspired men to write it. He inspires men to preach it. Jesus said of the Holy Spirit: "He shall glorify me." He honors Christ in the life of a dedicated and a consecrated believer. The Father honors Jesus. Jesus honors the Father. When John the Baptist came on the scene he honored Christ. He said, "He must increase, but I must decrease!" The Holy Spirit will always honor a message preached by any one when He magnifies Christ. John could say with boldness, "Behold the Lamb of God who taketh away the sin of the world." It always pleases and honors the Holy Spirit when we as children of God can truthfully say, "Christ shall be magnified in my body, whether it be by life or by death." Philippians 1:20.

THE HOLY SPIRIT WORKS IN PRAYER

The Holy Spirit impresses us as to what we should pray. "For we know not what we should pray for as we ought: but the Spirit himself maketh intercessions for us with groanings which cannot be uttered . . . for he maketh intercession for the saints according to the will of God." Romans 8:26-27. So often we hear people say, "I just can't seem to get through in my praying." It could be that you have not sought the leadership of the Spirit in your prayer life. He will not lead us to pray for things we do not need. He will not lead us to pray contrary to the will of God. He not only impresses us as to what we should pray for but He intercedes for us. He makes known the will of God for us. He will lead us into the doing of the will of God. He furnishes power for every divine assignment. "Not by might, *nor by power,* but by my Spirit saith the Lord of Hosts." Zechariah 4:6.

HE IS A SAFE AND AN ADEQUATE GUIDE

The Holy Spirit will call, fit, qualify and choose the place of work for the called, if he or she will let Him so do. Often there is more human effort than there is dependence upon the Spirit's leadership. He will put a preacher, missionary, or any other Christian where he ought to be when He guides them. Jesus told the disciples that when the Comforter would come He would guide them into all truth.

He will guide the Christian in his assigned task. He will give us wise counsel and guidance. He will furnish the power needed.

An old hymn expresses the thought that I have in mind.

"Holy Spirit, faithful guide,
Ever near the Christian's side,
Gently lead us by the hand,
Pilgrims in a desert land."

Marcus M. Wells

He will guide us in the sunshine and in the shadow hours. We all have the dark labyrinthian experiences in life. Jesus knew that we would need another Comforter for such experiences. Human suffering, and sorrow are common among people everywhere.

"While life's dark maize I tread,
And griefs around me spread,
Be Thou my guide;
Bid darkness turn to day,
Wipe sorrow's tears away,
Nor let me ever stray

115

From Thee aside."

Ray Palmer

The Holy Spirit will guide us and help us as we seek to win the lost. The New Testament bears out this fact. Our experiences as witnesses of what Jesus can do for a sinner confirm the fact that the Spirit will go before us and prepare the person for our coming. The early Christians "went from house to house" after the Spirit came upon them.

The book of Acts records the fact that they who were scattered abroad as a result of the persecution went everywhere preaching the Word. These witnessing Christians were filled with the Holy Spirit. They went out under the direction and inspiration of the Holy Spirit.

In the eighth chapter of Acts we have the record of a Christian layman being led by the Spirit to talk with a man from Ethiopia who had been to Jerusalem. He was reading in the 53rd. chapter of Isaiah. He did not understand it. God brought a saved man and a lost man together in a chariot. As a result of this meeting and the Spirit's working, a lost man was saved. He went on his way rejoicing, and no doubt he told others of what had happened to him.

In my experience as a Christian I have had victory over every difficulty in dealing with a lost person when I was absolutely sure that the Spirit of God was working at both ends of the line.

When we undertake something for God we need to be sure we are led by His Spirit. We need to pray,

"Spirit of the living God,
Fall fresh on me.
Break me, melt me,
Mold me, fill me.
Spirit of the living God,
Fall fresh on me."

CHAPTER FOURTEEN

GOD'S CALL TO REPENTANCE

"And the times of this ignorance God winked at: but now commandeth all men everywhere to repent:

Because he hath appointed a day, in which he will judge the world in righteousness by that man whom he hath ordained; whereof he hath given assurance unto all men, in that he hath raised him from the dead." Acts 17:30-31

One of the great and good men of my day said on one occasion, "The most patriotic thing we could do as a nation would be for us to repent of our sins."

God calls to individuals and to nations. He calls us to repent of our sins. It would take many chapters to list the sins for which we should ask God to forgive us as individuals and as a nation. It is much easier for us to think of the other man's sins than it is to face our own sins of omission and our sins of commission. It could be that much of the lawlessness of our day is the result of our sowing. Parents have indulged in sin. We have allowed the sale of liquor, the use of drugs, the desecration of the Sabbath, and immorality to go on without taking a firm stand against these things that will be the destruction of a nation.

God calls His people to repent of their sins. 2 Chronicles 7:14 is a fine illustration of what God expects of His people.

"If my people, which are called by my name, shall humble themselves, and pray, and seek my face, and turn from their wicked ways; then will I hear from heaven, and will forgive their sin, and will heal their land." In the words of the major and the minor prophets you will find that God calls over and over again for His people to forsake their sins and to turn again to Jehovah their God who is willing to forgive a penitent people.

GOD NOT ONLY CALLS TO REPENTANCE BUT HE COMMANDS IT

He calls because all are sinners. "For all have sinned and come short of the glory of God." "The heart is deceitful and desperately wicked, who can know it?" "All we like sheep have gone astray, we have turned every one unto his own way . . ." "And that repentance and remission of sin should be preached in his name among all nations."

There cannot be any salvation apart from genuine repentance. "Repentance toward God and faith in our Lord Jesus Christ" is a must for the sinner who needs to be saved and desires salvation. Jesus said, "Except ye repent ye shall all likewise perish . . ." Those who heard the Gospel preached on the day of Pentecost were pricked in their hearts and asked Peter and the rest of the Apostles, "Men and brethren, what shall we do? Then Peter said unto them, Repent, and be baptized every one of you in the name of Jesus Christ for the remission of sins, and ye shall receive the gift of the Holy Spirit." Acts 2:37-38

Every preacher should have repentance in his messages. There were many men of God spoken of in the Old Testament and in the New who called people of all walks of life to repentance. One who reads the Bible finds that Isaiah and Jeremiah called people to repent. Men like Amos and Hosea stressed the importance of repentance for personal and national sins. Noah and Jonah called upon the people to repent and to turn to God, seeking forgiveness for sins. John the Baptist came preaching repentance. When Jesus came in human flesh He called people to repent. He said very frankly and boldly — "Except ye repent ye shall all likewise perish." This means the rich and the poor, the mighty and the meek, the learned and the unlearned, and the black and the white; yea, all men everywhere.

Repentance is not only an act but a process. It is important for one to repent of his sins and put his trust in Jesus as Savior and Lord. Then, too, the sinner saved by grace must repent when he sins against God. God is not through with us when we accept salvation as a free gift from God.

THE MEANING OF REPENTANCE

There are those who say that repentance means to "quit your meanness". Surely the person who repents of sin will give up his evil habits. The prophet said in Isaiah 55:7, "Let the wicked forsake his way, and the unrighteous man his thoughts: and let him return unto the Lord, and he will have mercy upon him; and to our God, for he will abundantly pardon."

There are others who say that repentance means "reformation". These seem to feel that self-improvement or doing better is about all that is involved in repentance for sin. The truth of doing better and self-improvement is involved in the call of God to repentance. Paul enjoins us "To be transformed by the renewing of your mind . . ."

There are those who say "restitution" means repentance. This is good where it is possible for one to so do. So often one cannot really repent until after he has made restitution. Zacchaeus told Jesus that if he had wronged any person he would restore to that person four fold. He was not condemned for this. However, one could make good every

119

wrong and still be a lost sinner needing to repent and place his trust in Christ for salvation.

As a boy I heard preachers in revivals say, "Repentance is to 'about face' when you are on the wrong road and get on the right road." There is more to repentance than just turning around when you are on the wrong road and finding the right road. If this is repentance then the sinner would not need the Word of God and the Spirit to bring conviction for sin. God enables the sinner to repent. The prodigal had deep sorrow for his sins and then he said, "I will arise and go to my father . . ." In going to his father he was willing to confess his sins and ask for forgiveness.

Repentance is a godly sorrow for sin that brings about a changed heart, mind, and attitude toward sin and sinful habits. Repentance is an inner change which manifests itself outwardly. We should read carefully the third chapter of Matthew. Genuine repentance includes reformation, or quitting your meanness as well as restitution and an "about face".

"Repentance is to leave
The sins we have loved before,
And show that we in earnest grieve
By doing so no more."

"If we confess our sins, he is faithful and just to forgive us our sins, and to cleanse us from all unrighteousness." 1 John 1:9

"He that covereth his sin shall not prosper; but who so confesseth and forsaketh them shall have mercy." Proverbs 28:13

"Every good tree bringeth forth good fruit; but a corrupt tree bringeth forth evil fruit." Matthew 7:17.

GOD CALLS TO REPENTANCE IN VARIOUS WAYS

God calls in and through His goodness. "Not knowing

that the goodness of God leadeth thee to repentance?" Romans 2:4 God loves the good and the bad. He gives His blessings to the saved and to the lost. He bestows His great and good gifts upon the lovely and the unlovely. He does not deal with us according to what we deserve but according to our needs He ministers unto us. His goodness should provoke us to live for Him. God sends the rain and the sunshine upon the just and the unjust. It is strange that so many children whose parents are all the time doing so much for them, disregard this and bring shame and disgrace on them. It is stranger still how so many of God's creatures do so little to show their gratitude to Him for all of His rich blessings.

God calls in and through His merciful dealings with us. The Psalmist reminds us that God hath not dealt with us according to our sins, but as a father pitieth his children, so doth the Lord pity them that fear Him. Psalm 103 God hath brought us through wars, famines, sickness, and disasters. The people of Israel felt that when some great calamity befell them that God was calling to them. Should we not feel the same way?

God calls us to repent in and through His Providences. These are directive, corrective, and permissive. Can you think of how God brought you through some experience in life when it seemed dark and the future was uncertain? It could be that you made God certain promises if He would be gracious and bring you safely through. One day a storm struck in a part of the country where storms occur frequently. A wicked old man saw the tornado coming his way. He promised God that if He would spare his life and bring him through he would give his heart and life to Him. Great trees were uprooted. Almost everything in the wake of the tornado was destroyed. The old man was spared. He made good the promise which he had made to God.

GOD CALLS IN HIS JUDGMENTS

There are many judgments spoken of in the Bible. Down through the years God's judgments have been visited upon people because of their sins. This was true of the judgment in Noah's day when the people, all save eight, were destroyed in a flood. This was true when God called the people in the days of Abraham. God was willing to spare the people a judgment of fire and brimstone if they would turn from their sins. They did not repent, therefore, they were destroyed. Had the people in the days of Jonah not repented, then they would have been destroyed. God's judgment fell upon the Egyptians because of their sins and rebellion. There is a great White Throne judgment coming to all nations of the world. We will all be there on this great and notable day. "For we must all appear before the judgment seat of Christ." "It is appointed unto man once to die and after this the judgment." At that great day, "The wicked shall be turned into hell, and all the nations that forget God . . ." Psalm 9:17

The story is told of a man who had rejected God's goodness, His merciful and providential dealings. His wife was a devout Christian. She had said to her husband that God would bring him to repentance in some way. If his goodness failed then he would deal severely with him. The home had been blessed with one child, a little boy, the apple of their eyes. Little Jack fell sick and in a very short time was gone. The mother felt that this was it. At first the father was rebellious and questioned the goodness and love of God. When he looked at Jack's toys and clothes, and would see his little pals at play, a spirit of resentment would well up in his heart. In telling this story to his preacher friend, he said that he realized that God was calling to him in this manner. He came out of his lostness and sorrow to repent of His sins and to place his trust in Jesus Christ as Savior and Lord. Yes, it is true that God deals with us in severity! God's judgments are

122

always just and right.

How true that "Godly sorrow worketh repentance to salvation not to be repented of . . ." 2 Corinthians 7:10 Often God must crush us before He can crown us.

In Proverbs 29:1 we find some very significant words: "He, that being often reproved hardeneth his neck, shall suddenly be destroyed, and that without remedy." Jesus said, "I would, but ye would not."

GOD ALWAYS GIVES THE SINNER
TIME TO REPENT

The anti-deluvians were called to repent. They were given space and time to repent and they repented not. For one hundred and twenty years Noah warned the people of this day of impending doom and destruction. All of God's goodnesses availed little or nothing with the people who lived before the flood. "And God saw that the wickedness of man was great in the earth, and that every imagination of the thoughts of his heart was only evil continually." Genesis 6:5

God warned and called the people of Sodom and Gomorrah to righteous living. This could not be a reality without repentance toward God. Because of their sins and unwillingness to repent and turn to God the judgment of God in the way of fire and brimstone fell upon them and destroyed them.

Jesus told the story of the rich man who lived and fared well in his day materially and physically. He died and in hell lifted up his eyes. He had this world's goods but he lacked things that are eternal and do not perish. He had his time and chance to repent and be saved but he repented not. A poor beggar who lay at the gate of the rich man's house had greater riches than this man. "What shall a man be profited, if he shall gain the whole world, and lose his own soul? Or what shall a man give in exchange for his soul?" Matthew 16:26

The Ninevites were given a space and a time to repent. Jonah preached unto them, reluctantly, and they heard and heeded the call of God and repented and were spared impending doom and destruction. We are told that the Ninevites repented in "sackcloth and in ashes".

Jezebel who lived a wicked life, and died as she lived, was given a time to repent but she failed to do so. Jezebel was heartless and cruel. She influenced her husband who was King to do sinful acts against the people and before God. The Bible tells us that "she repented not".

How long did you have before you repented? Many people hear the call of God in youth and respond then. As a matter of fact, most of the people who are born of the Spirit and are regenerated have this experience in the years between 9 and 21. The number who are saved becomes fewer after people reach adulthood. The Junior years are the Golden years. "Remember now thy creator in the days of thy youth" is indeed a wise entreaty. We very often hear of some person dying suddenly and unexpectedly and people remark, "Isn't it too bad he was taken without warning?" I have known of some lost people meeting with sudden death when they were 40 or 50 years of age. God had given them many years in which to get right with God but they heeded not His call to come repenting and exercising faith in Christ. "The Spirit and the bride say, Come, and let him that heareth say, Come. And let him that is athrist come. And whosoever will, let him take of the water of life freely." Revelation 22:17 We are assured that "Whosoever shall call upon the name of the Lord shall be saved." The time for the lost sinner to turn in genuine repentance to God is when he feels the Spirit of God striving within. "Today is the day of salvation." "Now is the accepted time . . ." "If ye hear his voice harden not your heart." Waiting until tomorrow may be too late. One of the great and grave dangers for the sinner is to defer action on life's most vital matter, his salvation. God's Spirit will not always strive with man. There comes a time when God must give the sinner up.

AN ILLUSTRATION IN POINT

A pastor and preacher friend of mine was conducting a revival down in Louisiana. He was one of the best evangelists I have ever known. He had a warm and a compassionate heart. He could woo and win the lost to Christ when the Holy Spirit was working. A lawyer was sitting in the rear of the sanctuary leaning back in his chair as he had done often before. The preacher made a statement that he had not thought of making in preparing his sermon. It was this, "Did you know that God was going to hold you responsible for the time you take to make up your mind?" This statement hit home with this lawyer. He came forward trusting Christ in the forgiveness of his sins. God will indeed hold us accountable for the time we take to repent and trust Him.

CHAPTER FIFTEEN

THE FORGIVENESS OF SIN
Psalm 32, Psalm 51, Mark 2, and Luke 7:41-50

These scriptures present some very graphic and personal facts about the forgiveness of sin. The person who has felt the Divine forgiveness of sin should be a happy person. The Psalmist could say, "Blessed is he whose transgression is forgiven, whose sin is covered." The forgiven sinner should tell others what has been done for him. The Psalmist is willing to acknowledge his sin to God, and is unwilling to hide his sin from God (which no one can do). The forgiven sinner is at peace with God because his sins have all been forgiven. Any sinner whose sins are all forgiven, pardoned, and cleansed has indeed a new life and a new outlook on life. One of the best and most helpful Psalms on forgiveness, and all that is involved in it, is the 51st. Surely, the Psalmist felt that sin had brought to him a guilt for his sins, and a willingness to turn in true confession and repentance to God, who alone could forgive him.

THERE IS AN URGENT NEED FOR FORGIVENESS

This need is felt by the sinner because he feels quilty before God. "For all have sinned and come short of the glory

127

of God." "There is none good, no not one." "I was shapen in iniquity and in sin did my mother conceive me." "All we like sheep have gone astray; we have turned every one unto his own way." These are some of the many references in the Bible to the fact that man is a sinner and stands in need of a Savior. All stand condemned before God. Man in his sinful state is lost and God is seeking for him. God has a greater concern in and for man than man has in finding God. There cannot be any forgiveness of sin without confession of sin to God. We cannot have salvation as a free gift from God unless and until we have been willing to repent of sin and.put our faith in Jesus Christ and what He has done on the cross for us. In Proverbs 28:13 we read, "He that covereth his sins shall not prosper: but whoso confesseth and forsaketh them shall have mercy." In 1 John 1:9 we find this statement, "If we confess our sins, he is faithful and just to forgive us our sins, and to cleanse us from all unrighteousness." All sinners owe an impossible debt. None of us can pay that debt. Jesus, because he was sinless and God's offering for sin, paid this debt. Yet not any one of us can know and feel that our debt has been paid until we are willing to accept by faith what Jesus did for us on the cross. The forgiven sinner can joyfully sing, "Jesus paid it all, all to him I owe." How true it is that, "The wages of sin is death, but the gift of God is eternal life through Jesus Christ our Lord." Romans 6:23

THE MEANING OF FORGIVENESS

Forgiveness means to "cover". In Psalm 103:1-3 the idea is expressed — "Bless the Lord, O my soul: and all that is within me, bless his holy name, Bless the Lord, O my soul, and forget not all his benefits: Who forgiveth (covereth) all thine iniquities; who healeth all thy disease . . ." In Jeremiah 31:34 this idea of having our sins covered is stated: "I will forgive their iniquities . . ." The Apostle states this idea in

Romans 4:7: "Blessed are they whose sins are forgiven (covered)." Jesus spoke forgiveness to the man who had been brought to him by four men. They had faith that Jesus could heal, and were concerned enough in the man to bring him to Jesus. "Jesus seeing their faith said unto the sick of the palsy; Son, be of good cheer; thy sins be forgiven thee." Matthew 9:2

Forgiveness means cleansing. "The blood of Jesus Christ his son cleanseth us from all sin." David expressed in his sinfulness a desire to be washed and scrubbed so that the guilt, hurt, and stain of sin could be washed away. In his penitent prayer, he prayed: "Purge me with hissop, and I shall be clean: wash me, and I shall be whiter than snow." He called on God: "Wash me thoroughly from mine iniquity, and cleanse me from my sin." The prophet Isaiah in 1:18 says: "come now and let us reason together, saith the Lord: though your sins be as scarlet, they shall be as white as snow; though they be red like crimson, they shall be as wool." This idea of our sins being washed away is expressed in Relevation 1:5: "Unto him that loved us, and washed us from our sins in his own blood. And hath made us kings and priests unto God and his Father; to him be glory and dominion forever and ever. Amen."

Forgiveness also means to remove or to take away. In the Old Testament the scapegoat bore away the sins of the people into the wilderness. Of course, this was a symbolic removal of sin from the guilty to the innocent. This pointed toward the day and the time when Jesus the Lamb of God would bear our sins on the cross in His own body. Those whose sins are forgiven can sing – "All my sins are taken away." And, too, they can sing the old hymn,

"At the cross, at the cross
Where I first saw the light,
And the burden of my heart rolled away,

129

It was there by faith
I received my sight,
And now I am happy all the day."

We are told in the Scripture that our sins are cast into the depth of the sea. Again we have a picture of our sins being removed from us as far as the east is from the west. Both of these references are symbols of our sins being removed far from us. Jesus took our sins away when He bore them on the cross. He who had done no sin became sin for us. This was done in order that we might be made righteous.

Only God can loose one from the bondage and fetters of sin. We are in bondage to sin and cannot free ourselves. The Demoniac is a picture of how man in bondage to sin is a slave to sin and cannot by any means or methods free himself. In Luke 8:26-39 Jesus relates a story of the man in Gadara who was demon possessed. Jesus healed the man and forgave his sins and told him to go and tell or show to his own house what great things the Lord had done for him.

Over and over again did I hear some of the men in our church when I was growing up, pray: "O God have mercy upon us and pardon all of our sins." It is altogether fitting for us to ask God to forgive and to pardon our iniquities. There is a legal aspect in pardon. When a person accused of some crime is given a pardon by the governor of the state in which he is serving time that man is set free when he accepts the pardon. It is not forced upon him. In Nehemiah 9:17 we find these words: "But thou art a God ready to pardon, gracious, and merciful."

In Numbers 14:19 are these words: "Pardon, I beseech thee, the iniquity of this people." In 2 Chronicles 30:18 Hezekiah prayed, saying, "The good Lord pardon everyone." Isaiah 55:7 enjoins the wicked, "Let the wicked forsake his way, and the unrighteous man his thoughts: and let him return unto the Lord, and he will have mercy upon him: and

130

to our God, for he will abundantly pardon." To every forgiven sinner God grants a pardon.

Forgiveness means to blot out. God erases, expunges, and wipes the slate clean when He forgives us. This man does not do. This man cannot do. God cannot take away the harm and the hurt of sin. The scars made by sin will follow us to the grave. There are many broken hearts, homes and lives left in the wake of sin. Isaiah 43:25 expresses this idea, "I, even I, am he that blotteth out thy transgressions, for mine own sake, and will not remember thy sins."

In Isaiah 44:22 we find this idea — "I have blotted out, as a thick cloud, thy transgressions, and as a cloud, thy sins: return unto me, for I have redeemed thee." In Psalm 51:1 the penitent sinner prays, "According unto the multitude of thy tender mercies, blot out my transgressions."

SOME EXAMPLES OF FORGIVENESS

In John 8:1-11 the story is told of a woman who was a sinner. She had been accused of living in adultery. The disciples accused her to the Master. According to the law of Moses such a person was guilty of death. We do not know what Jesus wrote on the ground, but He said to them, "He that is without sin among you, let him first cast a stone at her." As He wrote again on the ground the accused were guilt conscious and they went away. When Jesus got up He said, "Woman, where are those thine accusers? Hath no man condemned thee? She said, No man, Lord. And Jesus said unto her, Neither do I condemn thee: go and sin no more." Had the woman been unwilling to live according to the purpose of God for a forgiven life then she would not have been forgiven.

In Mark 2:1-12 is a story about the healing of a man who had been palsied for many years. Four men with great difficulty brought this man to Jesus. He needed his body

131

healed. However, his greatest need was for his sins to be forgiven. The men who brought him to Jesus had faith in Jesus. Jesus saw the man's need and that beyond his physical need was his need for the forgiveness of sin. No doubt most of the crowd present saw only the physical need of the man. Jesus said to him, "Son, thy sins be forgiven thee." It was following this that Jesus said, "I say unto thee, arise and take up thy bed, and go into thine house.

And immediately he arose, took up his bed, and went forth before them all; insomuch that they were all amazed, and glorified God, saying we never saw it on this fashion."

THE PRODIGAL SON WAS FORGIVEN OF HIS SINS

The interesting story of how the prodigal son was forgiven of his sins is found in Luke 15:11-32. We find many facts in this simple human interest story that applies to the prodigal sons and daughters of our day. He took his departure into a far country. He lived a life of waste. The record tells us that he spent his substance in riotous living. When he had spent all he came to himself. In fact, he did not come to himself until he was in dire need. It was then that he thought of home and resolved to go back home. He resolved to confess his sins to his father and to be made as a hired servant. It seems that this wayward son was conscious of his sin against his father, against God, and against himself. This he confessed in shame and in humility. He said, "Father, I have sinned against heaven, and in thy sight." We see the father and son meeting. The father was willing to forgive his wayward son. The son was willing to confess and to forsake his sins as the father bestowed his joy and love upon him. With his sins forgiven the son could again enjoy the fellowship of his home and his father. God is always ready and willing to forgive any and all sinners who come to Him seeking forgiveness. It does not take a seeking sinner and a seeking Savior long to get together. Every sinner saved by grace knows the joy that comes when Jesus says, "Son, thy sins are all forgiven."

CHAPTER SIXTEEN

THE ELEMENT OF SACRIFICE IN LIFE

"Then said Jesus unto his disciples, If any man will come after me, let me deny himself, and take up his cross, and follow me. For whosoever shall save his life shall lose it: and whosoever shall lose his life for my sake shall find it." Matthew 16:24-25.

On another occasion Jesus said, "Except a corn of wheat fall into the ground and die, it abideth alone: but if it die, it bringeth forth much fruit." John 12:24

One of life's paradoxies is we must die to live. The way grain can live is to die. The farmer throws away much grain, which dies, but look at the harvest he reaps because the grain that was sowed, dies. There is a sacrifice that is loss and there is a sacrifice that is gain. Not all sacrifices are acceptable to God. "They sacrifice . . . but the Lord accepteth them not." Hosea 8:13 All over the world there are various interpretations of sacrifice. There are conflicting notions about what is involved.

THERE ARE SEVERAL KINDS OF SACRIFICE

There is the instinctive type of sacrifice. The mother bird will fly into the mouth of a serpent seeking to protect her young. There is a great deal of this in the life of birds and fowls. There is much of this in the lower animal kingdom.

There is the unconscious type of sacrifice. Daily animals are dying for us. Fish, fowls, cows, sheep, swine, and other animals are dying so that we may have food. In the vegetable kingdom tons upon tons of nice fresh vegetables are consumed by us. This unconscious type of sacrifice helps to keep our bodies nourished and fed.

There is the involuntary type of sacrifice. This is found in many areas of life. It is reflected in forced military service. It is seen in "Death Marches" and in "concentration camps". Thousands have died in such situations over which they had no control and in which they literally died. It is a matter of record that one railroad under construction cost one hundred thousand lives. During the construction of the Panama Canal 32,000 men died from fever and other causes.

Millions of people have died during war. More than two million people died from cold and hunger in and around Stalingrad during World War II. It would be difficult to tell how many people died from exposure and hunger and otherwise in World Wars I and II. Millions died who could not help it. This to many was useless sacrifice of human lives.

There is the voluntary type of sacrifice. This is the finest and the highest type of sacrifice. Great numbers of people lay down their lives in some great cause. They do this willingly and voluntarily. Many brave men have laid themselves upon the altar as a sacrifice for the cause of freedom and that which they believed to be right. Many men and women have given themselves to the cause of missions. This called for the leaving of loved ones and country to go out where the going was difficult and exacting. They have been willing to die or to "burn out" for God. The apostle could say, "I die daily."

Jesus is the finest example of one dying voluntarily for a great purpose and cause. He said, "I lay down my life that I might take it again", and again "No man can take it from

134

me." His enemies said of Him, "He saved others, himself he cannot save." Jesus did not die because He could not help it. He did not die the death of a martyr. He gave Himself as a ransom for our sins. He who knew no sin, became sin for us that we might be made the righteousness of God in Him. There is a saying that is packed with meaning, "Jesus will put his blood as far as we put ours". If we would bless others we must be willing to bleed for the cause of Christ.

THE ELEMENT OF SACRIFICE IS FOUND IN ALL RELIGIONS

Sacrifice is found in Confucianism. The people who subscribe to this religion go through rather rigid practices of self-denial and self-renunciation. Many who hold to this religion are willing to give up all in the interest of their religion.

The element of sacrifice is very pronounced in Buddhism. Much of this is fatalism. People are willing to be burned up for what they believe to be right. This has been seen in human torches in Viet Nam. Suicide squads have attached high explosives to their bodies and have attacked a ship or a convoy when they knew this would mean sudden death. These were called "suicide squads".

Hinduism also has a very definitive element of sacrifice in it. Often the body is tortured to appease their god. Some will walk through burning coals or lie down on sharp spikes, doing what they think will satisfy their god. Widows are burned at the stake or killed. Children are thrown into the river and drowned to satisfy and appease an angry god.

Judaism, too, has the thread of sacrifices all through the Old Testament. In the early history of man the innocent victim was slain to provide a covering for Adam and Eve who had sinned against God. Genesis 3:21 Later people slew their children (2 Kings 23:10 and Jeremiah 32:35). The Lamb was

135

slain in Egypt and the blood was sprinkled on the lintels of the doors to show that they were safe under the blood. God had said, "When I see the blood, I will pass over you . . ." Exodus 12:13. The ceremony of laying the sins of the people on the scapegoat denoted the innocent bearing the sins of the guilty. Sacrifice is enunciated in the five great offerings spoken of in Leviticus chapters one through five.

The element of sacrifice is vital and essential in Christianity. This is set forth in the slaying of the lamb for the Passover meal. It was the lamb without spot and without blemish that "takes away sin". John the Baptist could truthfully say, "Behold the Lamb of God, who taketh away the sin of the world." Isaiah 53 gives us a vivid picture of the suffering servant who is none other than Jesus. Atonement for sin was provided for in the death of Jesus, God's only begotten son, "Without shedding of blood is no remission . . ." Hebrews 9:22 John in 1 John 1:7 speaks, "The blood of Jesus Christ his son cleanseth us from all sin." Jesus said, "Except a grain of wheat fall into the ground and die it abideth alone."

SACRIFICE IS ESSENTIAL IN THE
CHRISTIAN LIFE

This fact should be reflected in our living. Someone has said, "That man lives twice who lives the first life well." In 2 Corinthians 5:15 is stated a great principle: "And that he died for all, that they who live should not henceforth live unto themselves, but unto him who died for them, and rose again." Paul could say, "I am crucified with Christ: nevertheless I live: . . . and the life which I now live in the flesh I live by the faith of the son of God, who loved me and gave himself for me." Galatians 2:20 Paul could say, "Christ liveth in me." When missionary Henry Martin went out to his mission field he said, "Now let me burn out for

God." This he did. Every true child of God should be able to say,

> "Lord, let me live from day to day,
> In such a self-forgetful way,
> That even when I kneel to pray,
> My prayer shall be for others."

We should be willing to render sacrificial services to God and to our fellowman. Our best example of this is Jesus "who came not to be ministered unto, but to minister, and to give his life a ransom for many". Many people are trying to squeeze out of life all they can. Others have learned the secret of abundant living. Jesus told his disciples that if they would be great they must be willing to be a servant. Carey worked in Burma for seven years before he had one convert to Christianity. Think of the lasting work in Burma and India which was begun by this man of God.

People need the challenge of a difficult task. Garibaldi of Italy in another day challenged the youth of his country by saying, "I do not offer you pay, provisions, or quarters. I offer hunger, thirst, forced marches, battles and death."

The spirit of sacrifice should be reflected in our giving. It is difficult to separate living, serving, and giving. These are all essential in the Christian life. A young doctor volunteered for mission work. He was offered a lucrative salary to stay at home and work. He said, "Your salary is all right, but your job is not big enough." He realized that the Kingdom of God is the greatest business in the world.

How many of us give as little as we can? How many give as we are able and go beyond the demands of the law? David is a good example of one who did not want to do as little as he could for his God. Another man was willing to provide him with a large gift which he could make. However, he said, "Neither will I offer burnt offerings unto the Lord my God of that which doth cost me nothing . . ." 2 Samuel 24:18-25

Cain and Abel were brothers and both made offerings to God. One was accepted while the offering of the other did not please God. Read Hebrews 11:4, "By faith Abel offered unto God a more excellent sacrifice than Cain, by which he obtained witness that he was righteous, God testifying of his gifts; and by it he being dead yet speaketh."

Dr. James P. Boyce, a native South Carolinian, was the founder of the Southern Baptist Seminary now located in Louisville, Kentucky. He put himself, his service, and money into this cause which seemed doomed during the Civil War. If the Seminary must die, he felt that he would die first. He put his blood into this great institution which has trained thousands of ministers and missionaries through the years. The spirit of such a man is catching.

When Cyrus Hamlin was a small boy he learned one of life's great lessons. His mother gave him seven cents to buy cookies and to give to missions. The money would not divide evenly so he gave it all to missions and went home hungry. Later he went as a missionary to Constantinople. He founded Roberts College. He invested his life in Turkey. In youth he learned that the real joy in life is not in getting, but in giving. He learned the great lesson of sharing the good news with others. Surely every Christian is willing or should be willing to show the spirit of sacrifice in his life, in his ministry, and in his giving.

138

CHAPTER SEVENTEEN

THE LORDSHIP OF JESUS

"Therefore let all the house of Israel know assuredly, that God hath made that same Jesus, whom ye have crucified, both Lord and Christ." Acts 2:36

On the day of Pentecost Peter stood up to preach. The theme of his sermon was "The Lordship of Jesus". Jesus had been crucified and had recently come forth from the grave. Great power was manifested in the hearts and lives of the disciples. They who believed in Christ went out everywhere witnessing concerning Jesus and His claims. People were saved and great numbers were added to the church as a result of their new found faith in Jesus as Savior and Lord. Peter without fear or favor declared the absolute Lordship of Jesus whom his enemies had rejected and crucified.

THE MEANING OF THE WORD "LORD"

The word "Lord" has reference to the "slave owner". In some places and in some lands the husband is addressed as "my lord". It is also a title of respect and honor. In England the mayor of a city is referred to as the "Lord Mayor". The owner of large lands is thought of as "Lord", or as the Land-lord. Governments in some places bestow this title upon some whom the government honors.

139

In the English Bible Lord is used in reference to Deity — God and Jesus. Thomas addressed Jesus, "My Lord and my God". When the crowds were leaving Jesus, he asked the disciples, "Will ye also go away?" Peter replied, "Lord, to whom shall we go?" In Revelation 19:16 Jesus is referred to as "King of Kings and Lord of Lords". On one occasion Jesus asked the very personal question, "Why do you call me Lord, Lord, and do not the things that I say?" Jesus is referred to in the New Testament twenty-three times as Savior. There are 430 references to Jesus as Lord. The evangel, John, proclaims the Absolute Lordship of Jesus Christ.

THE GROUNDS OR BASES FOR HIS LORDSHIP

The Deity of Jesus is foundational in the Lordship of Jesus. He and the Father are one. He is co-existent with the Father. Before Abraham was, He existed. He was before the foundation of the world. John in his prologue sets forth the fact that Jesus was with God in the beginning. "In the beginning was the Word, and the Word was with God, and the Word was God. The same was in the beginning with God." John 1:1-2

His relation to the law is also basic in His claim to be Lord of all. He is the end of the law. He did not come to destroy the law but to fill it full of richer meaning. He said to His disciples, "Think not that I am come to destroy the law, or the prophets: I am not come to destroy, but to fulfill. For verily I say unto you, till heaven and earth pass, one jot or one tittle shall in no wise pass from the law, till all be fulfilled." Matthew 5:17-18 Jesus had profound respect for the law and gave richer meaning to it. He is the highest end and fulfillment of the law. In the two great commandments which He gave, all the law and the prophets are fulfilled when these are fully kept. We are to love God with all our faculties and love our neighbor as we love ourselves.

Jesus and His Lordship are reflected in creation. He was there in the beginning with God. Paul tells us that nothing that was made, was made without Him. He also reminds us that "in Him all things consist or hold together." He is the great magnet which holds things together today.

Jesus is Lord over the New Creation. Someone has rightfully said, "He is Savior in His Lordship, and He is Lord in His Saviorship." How can any person be willing to accept Jesus as Savior and refuse to make Him Lord in and over his life? If Jesus is not made Lord in one's life then He cannot be one's Savior. In 2 Corinthians 5:17 we find a great principle stated: "Therefore if any man be in Christ, he is a new creature: old things are passed away; behold all things are become new." Time and time again Jesus said we were to have only one master. We are not our own. We belong to God in Christ. He bought us. Since we belong to Christ we are to honor and glorify Him. We are to be subject to Him.

Jesus has a right to be Lord because all power belongs to Him. "Jesus came and spake unto them saying, All power is given unto me in Heaven and in earth. Go ye therefore, and teach all nations, baptizing them in the name of the Father, and of the Son, and of the Holy Spirit: Teaching them to observe all things whatsoever I have commanded you: and lo, I am with you alway, even unto the end of the world." Matthew 28:18-20 In this scripture is found our commission. It also assures us that we are under Divine command to go to all people of the earth with a message rooted in the Saviorship and the Lordship of Jesus Christ.

Jesus has a right to be Lord because of who He is, what He has done, and what He is now doing. He is not only God's only Son, but He is God revealed to us in human flesh. "God hath made that same Jesus whom ye have crucified both Lord and Christ" was preached by Peter. God honored the sermon in bringing multitudes of people to trust in Jesus and to a willingness to follow Jesus in New Testament baptism, and to the homes of people who needed salvation. Read Philippians 2:1-5.

THE AREAS IN WHICH JESUS HAS
A RIGHT TO BE LORD

He has a right to be made Lord in every heart of every true believer. We sing a meaningful little chorus, "Into my heart, into my heart, come into my heart Lord Jesus. Come in today, come in to stay. Come into my heart Lord Jesus." In all things Christ should have the pre-emience. Jesus said that not all who called Him Lord, Lord would enter into the Kingdom, but those who did the will of God. The story is told of a fine young woman who wore a locket with the words written in it: "Whom having not seen I love".

He has a right to be Lord in your social life. As a matter of fact, this is often the place where we are tempted and tried the most. If Jesus cannot be Lord in your social life then He will not be Lord at all. So often Christ is crucified in the homes of His so-called friends. How true it is, "That this vile world is not a friend to grace, to help us on to God."

Jesus has a right to be Lord in the home. What would your community be like if every home were truly Christian? Every child has a right to have the blessings of a Christian home. So many are robbed of this. It is not strange that we have so much lawlessness and juvenile delinquency today. There is a lack of wholesomeness in many homes; a lack of Bible study and prayer on the part of the family. There is a failure to worship in some good church where the home can have the help and encouragement of the church. We need all the help we can get today to save our homes. We cannot "train up a child in the way he should go", without Christian examples and teachings. A boy who had broken many laws and was before the judge for some crime was asked if he had anything to say. He replied, "Judge, I need some new parents." All parents need new hearts and a firm faith in God to do their job worthily and well. The Psalmist in 127:1 says, "Except the Lord build the house, they labor in vain that build it: except the Lord keep the city, the watchman waketh but in vain." How true this is!

The Lordship of Jesus should be a reality in His church. Many great doctrines of the Bible are rooted in the Lordship of Jesus. Since Jesus is responsible for the church, He has a right to expect His church to make Him Lord. He not only is the founder of the church, but He is the head of the church. He is the founder and the foundation of the church. The members of the church belong to Christ. The church is the pillar and the ground of the truth. He loved the church and gave Himself for her. So ought we to love the church and give ourselves for her well-being. "His slightest wish" should be our greatest delight. "Christ courts no man. He commands all men."

If Jesus is Lord in all of life then His followers can truthfully sing,

"All hail the power of Jesus name!
Let angels prostrate fall;
Bring forth the royal diadem,
And crown Him Lord of all."

CHAPTER EIGHTEEN

ESSENTIALS IN CHRISTIAN CHARACTER

"A good name is rather to be chosen than great riches, and loving favor rather than silver and gold." Proverbs 22:1

"Other foundations can no man lay than that is laid, Christ Jesus." 1 Corinthians 3:11

"For we are his workmanship, created in Christ Jesus unto good works . . ." Ephesians 2:10

Character is what you are in thought, heart, life, and habit. It is what one really is in his very life and nature. Character is one's greatest collateral. If you have cash and do not have genuine character, you do not have much. If you have character you can get some cash. Reputation is what people think of you. It may be good or bad. Character is the sum total of all your habits. Habit economizes energy and makes us more efficient than we could be otherwise. Jesus said, "A man's life consisteth not in the abundance of the things which he possesseth."

LAYING THE RIGHT KIND OF FOUNDATION

It is essential for one to lay the right kind of foundation upon which to build. We cannot afford to economize on the foundation in building a home or a great office building or any other kind of building. Heredity is important in character building. Psychologists tell us that heredity is of vital importance in producing the right kind of person or character. Children should be well born. Millions are brought into this world without ever having a fair chance. So many are born in poverty, ignorance, and with the curse of their parents upon them. Surely, no informed person will fail to realize the place that heredity plays in the life of a child.

The right kind of environment is essential in the life of a child. It is almost impossible to find noble Christian men and women coming out of the Ghettos. They have breathed the germs of sin and disease so long that it is impossible to live in such an evil environment and be strong in Christian convictions and character. Over and over again people with Christian experiences have said, "If I am to live right then I must get out of the environment in which I am now living." Often I have thought of boys and girls who have been won to the Christian faith who find it almost impossible to live a decent life in the kind of environment in which they live in the home and in the community. Even the government is beginning to realize this fact and are trying to do something about the infested environments in which millions live. Such environments breed disease, crime, and poverty. A good healthy, wholesome environment is essential in character development. There is a deadly "fall-out" in our cities and in many other places. Millions of children are doomed and damned from birth.

Teaching and training of the right kind are essential in Christian character.

"Sow a thought and reap an act,
Sow an act and reap a habit,
Sow a habit and reap a character,
Sow a character and reap a destiny."

In Proverbs 22:6 we find an oft quoted

146

statement: "Train up a child in the way he should go: and when he is old, he will not depart from it." Often we fail to realize that we as parents have failed to train a child in the way he should go. Many go their own ways and we do not direct them in the right way. Then we often overlook the pull of influences outside the Christian home that cause our children to depart from the faith. The pull of the world on young and old is very strong. To teach our children, from day to day, should be done with consistency. In many so-called homes there is not enough Bible instruction, prayer, and wise counsel. Jesus sets forth some great teachings in the Sermon on the Mount. At the conclusion of this masterpiece He says, "Whosoever heareth these sayings of mine, and doeth them, I will liken him unto a wise man, which built his house upon a rock: And the rain descended, and the floods came, and the winds blew, and beat upon that house; and it fell not: for it was founded upon a rock." Matthew 7:24-25 In explaining the parable of the sower Jesus tells that the seed which fell by the wayside and were devoured by the birds was the word which was heard by some and the devil came and took it away. The devil is still seeking to nullify the Word when it falls upon the mind of the hearer.

WE SHOULD USE THE RIGHT KIND OF
MATERIAL IN CHARACTER BUILDING

Jesus Christ is a safe and a secure foundation upon which life can be laid. Paul laid a foundation as a wise master builder. "Other foundation can no man lay, than that which is laid, Christ Jesus." We are indeed God's building. We are God's husbandry. A personal, saving faith in Christ is essential in Christian character. We are to take heed as to how we build thereupon. It is never wise to economize on foundations. The story is told of a great cement plant at Hudson, New York literally sinking into the ground and

147

disappearing. Upon investigation it was found that the plant had been built on what appeared to be a good clay foundation but actually was built on sinking sand. Many people are building upon sinking sand.

> "My hope is built on nothing less
> Than Jesus' blood and righteousness:
> I dare not trust the sweetest frame,
> But wholly lean on Jesus' name.
> On Christ, the solid Rock, I stand:
> All other ground is sinking sand."

Christ indeed is the Solid Rock on which we can safely build our lives.

The right kind of choices are most important. We cannot serve two masters. Our choices affect our characters. Our choice of friends often determines our destinies in time and in eternity. These can point us toward the upper road or to the road that leads to destruction. The choice of our life's work will have much to do with what we become in life.

The right kind of habits will have much to do with the development of our characters. Longfellow in "The Builders" utters a wise word:

> "All are architects of fate,
> Working within these massive walls of time;
> Make the house where God may dwell,
> Beautiful, entire, and clean."

Every day we are strengthening or we are weakening our character. It would be most helpful to have a daily devotional period. At this time you can meet God and in Bible study and prayer you will be given strength for the day. Every person needs to worship God. We should avail ourselves of this fine and enriching opportunity. Practice daily the presence of God. Isaiah 40:31 utters a wise word: "And they that wait upon the Lord shall renew their strength; they shall mount up with wings as eagles, they shall run, and not be weary, and they shall walk, and not faint." Jesus tells us to watch and pray lest we enter into temptation. In one of our hymns of praise and worship we sing, "Take time to be holy, speak oft with thy Lord . . . abide in him always . . . and feed on his word."

In character building we should have a noble and a worthy purpose in life. It is important for us to ask, Why am I here? Where am I going? What am I proposing and purposing to do with my life? There are too many drifters and floaters in life. Many people have never discovered a serious purpose in life. Life is meaningless for those who are aimless and purposeless. Daniel had a purpose in life. Jesus' purpose was to do the will of His Father and to finish His work. When Pilgrim left the city of destruction he headed toward "Yon Wicket Gate". He left the city of destruction and moved toward the City of God. Paul pressed toward the mark for the high calling of God in Christ Jesus.

We should have deep convictions based on truth and have the courage to live by them. Convictions, courage, and consistency in living the Christian life are most essential. We need to know when to say "No"! We also need to know when to say "Yes!" There are many spineless people. John the Baptist had convictions and he had courage to stand with such convictions. Jesus in appraising him said, "Of those born of woman, there hath not arisen a greater than John the Baptist." There are many people who are willing to fight and to die for their convictions even when they are wrong. Peter and John had courage to stand by their convictions for they were sure that they were right. They must obey God rather than man. In a crucial hour Martin Luther said, "Here I stand, God being my helper, I can do none other." When John Bunyan was in jail for preaching the Gospel he said, "I will stay here until moss grows on my brow before I will make a slaughterhouse of my conscience."

SOME OF THE AREAS WHERE CHARACTER
IS TESTED

There are many areas in which we are tested and tried. Someone has said that there are four persons in this corporal body. There is the person I know myself to be. There are some things about the most of us that no one else knows. There is the person my family knows me to be. There is the person that my business associates and competitors know me to be. Then there is the person that God knows me to be. When we are selecting a photo from several that have been made of us, we pick out the one that flatters us the most. Then many will say, "That is not the best likeness of me." It could be that if we had the best likeness of what we are, it would still not look so good.

The home test is a good one. We should be at our best in our homes. It is my conviction that if Christianity does not make us act right in the home we cannot justify seeking to pass it on to others. Many of life's greatest lessons are caught in the home because they are taught by example. I have known some people who reveal the ugly side of life in the home.

There is the business test of character. Have you ever left home with a sour and grouchy feeling and gone into the office with a smile and a happy outlook on the day? Have you ever shown the best side in the office and the "fussy" side at home? I read of a man who often criticized people rather severely. He decided to do some bragging on people that waited on him in the grocery store and at other places. This practice changed him and those with whom he did business.

There is the social test. What is your attitude toward people when you enjoy social advantages that others know not? We never rise any higher in our Christian lives than in our social activities. Martha Berry, founder of Berry College

150

in Georgia, had wealth and social prestige. She decided to invest her life in helping others who were less fortunate than she. She has blessed great numbers of young people in the college which she founded.

There is the success test. Often favoring circumstances bring wealth to some and this is considered success. Others have great political power and prestige. Character is tested when great honors are bestowed. Many accept such honors with humility and never lose touch with the plain and simple people who never know fame and fortune.

The story is told of a young man who graduated from college with one of the highest honors the college offered. Before the medal of honor was presented to this young man, the President had many fine things to say about him. The boy had denied himself of many things in order that he might receive a college education. However, someone else had borne the burden in this young man's attainment. Sitting in the audience was the proud mother of this honored young man. She had literally put her blood into her son. She had looked forward to the day when her son would graduate from college. When the son received the medal of honor with gratitude and with deep appreciation, he walked off the stage and down to where his mother sat and pinned the medal on her saying, "Mother, you deserve this medal more than I do." People were greatly moved as they witnessed the deep devotion of this son to his mother who had sacrificed so many things in order that he might have and enjoy advantages that she never knew.

CHAPTER NINETEEN

THE MEASURE AND THE MEANING
OF FAITH

"And now abideth faith, hope, and love, these three; but the greatest of these is love." 1 Corinthians 13:13

"But without faith it is impossible to please Him." Hebrews 11:6

"Faith is the substance of things hoped for, the evidence of things not seen." Hebrews 11:1

It is good to know in this day when things are changing so rapidly that there are some things that abide. God does not change. His inspired Word does not change. When things all about us are giving way and are changing we can be anchored in the eternal things of God. In my day history books, geography, and science have all been changed. If we have faith in God we take Him at His word. To doubt the Word is to question the integrity of God. No person can exercise saving faith apart from a personal faith in Christ as Savior and Lord. Jesus came into the world to make God known to man. No person has seen God apart from Jesus. Without faith we cannot know God. Without faith we cannot lay hold upon God's promises that deal with that which lies beyond. Too many have misplaced their faith. Someone said, "I do not have much faith in the future, but I do have faith in the God who knows the future." *Faith is fundamental in the Christian faith.* We can limit God in our lives by our lack of faith. Let us consider some things about the measure and meaning of faith.

THERE IS A SAVING FAITH

No person can be a Christian apart from faith (belief and trust) in Jesus as a personal Savior. This statement will run into difficulty with those who do not believe in the necessity of faith in salvation. No person can feel like a Christian who has not had a personal encounter with Christ. Jesus healed a woman with "an issue of blood". He said to this woman, "Daughter, be of good comfort; thy faith hath made thee whole." Matthew 9:22 Faith is the means whereby we appropriate what grace has provided. To believe, to trust, to confide in, are all wrapped up in genuine faith in Christ. Faith in laws, dogmas, works, our goodness, and our prayers will not save us. It is faith in the person of Jesus Christ.

Genuine faith in Christ will lead the lost sinner to repentance. It is not possible for us to separate faith from repentance. Each is essential to the other. Faith in a person begins with belief in the facts about that person. "Faith cometh by hearing, and hearing by the word of God." Faith is not an arbitrary matter. Forgiveness comes through faith. Faith is a titled deed assuring us of eternal life in Jesus Christ.

THERE IS A WORKING FAITH

Faith is to be active and not passive. For one who is saved to be idle, and do nothing to show that he has been saved, is a misrepresentation of the fact of faith. In Philippians 2:12-13 this principle of faith is shown at work. "Wherefore, my beloved, as ye have always obeyed, not as in my presence only, but now much more in my absence, work out your own salvation with fear and trembling. For it is God who worketh in you both to will and to do of his good pleasure." In the teachings of Paul and James there is no conflict. Each expresses in his own way how we show our faith in and through our works. James very plainly says, "For as the body without the spirit is dead, so faith without works is dead also. James 2:26

If the farmer did not have faith in the seasons he would not keep on sowing and planting seed. It takes a working faith to get things done. If we did not have faith in God we would not keep on working for Him, even though the day may be dark, trying, discouraging, and often disappointing. Faith keeps us moving on in the work to which we have been called. It takes faith to claim the promises of God. There is an old saying that has a great truth in it:

"The best of all the preachers is the man who lives his creeds,

For to see the good in action is what everybody needs."

In Galatians 2:16 Paul makes a timely statement: "Knowing that a man is not justified by the works of the law, but by the faith of Jesus Christ, even we have believed in Jesus Christ, that we might be justified by the faith of Christ, and not by the works of the law: for by the works of the law shall no flesh be justified." In Galatians 3:11 the Apostle says, "The just shall live by faith." The works of the just show that he lives, and because he lives he works.

In the Scriptures we find that we are to "work out" our salvation. This does not mean that we are to work in order that we might be saved. We are to work because we are saved. We cannot be strong and virile Christians without a certain amount of spiritual exercise. Growing flowers, a garden, or a crop calls for work. The soil must be prepared. The seed or plants must be placed in the ground. Then, we are to "work out" that which we have planted. If we fail at this point, then weeds, grass, etc. will destroy that which we have placed in the ground. To be consistent we, as Christians, are to work in the Kingdom of God. We say by our works that we have been saved and delight to work because we are saved. A workless church member is a useless and a fruitless church member. Mr. Lowell once said, "No man without intense faith in something can ever be in earnest." James said, ". . . Show me thy faith without thy works, and I will show thee my faith by my works."

THE WALK OF FAITH

Some people do not walk "as becometh the children of God". There is a walk of faith that each of us must take. In 2 Corinthians 5:7 we read, "For we walk by faith, not by sight." None of us can see to the end of the road or the path over which we travel daily. In driving a car at night there is light sufficient to drive on over the smooth and the straight, and even the curves in the road. We move out and on and the light of the car lights the road. So often people make the remark, "I wish I knew what lies out at the end of the year or beyond." If we knew what awaits us, we would likely pray that God would just make it known as we come to it. Grace is provided for us daily each step of the way. The walk of Abraham was a walk of faith. He took God at His word and went into a land that he had never seen. This took faith. He obeyed, and went out, not knowing where he was to go. He looked for a city whose maker and builder was God. Noah had faith in God. He built an ark by faith. He prepared an ark to the saving of his people. Day by day he walked and had fellowship with God. We know that the just shall live by faith. They must also walk by faith in God. A storm was raging at sea. A small boy riding on the boat seemed not to be afraid. Someone asked him if he were not afraid. He replied, "My father is at the helm." When men of God walk

156

with God through the calm and through the storm there is no need for fear.

Moses also had faith to trust God and to follow him through all of the journey over which he was to travel, in wilderness, in desert, and across the sea. Here is a man who in many trying conditions and circumstances trusted in God and walked on with Him. "Esteeming the reproaches of Christ greater riches than the treasures in Egypt; for he had respect unto the recompense of the reward." Hebrews 11:6 A religious skeptic on a college campus said of an ardent Christian, "I can answer his arguments, but I cannot answer his life." John says, "But if we walk in the light, as he is in the light, we have fellowship one with another, and the blood of Jesus Christ his son cleanseth us from all sin." In Ephesians we read, "Be ye therefore followers of God, as dear children; And walk in love, as Christ also hath loved us, and hath given himself for us an offering and a sacrifice to God for a sweet smelling savor." Ephesians 5:1-2

FAITH IN THE GOSPEL

The Gospel is good news. Paul speaks of the Gospel as being "the power of God unto salvation to every one that believeth; to the Jew first, and also to the Greek." Romans 1:16 We are enjoined in Philippians 1:27-30 "Only let your conversation be as it becometh the Gospel of Christ: that whether I come and see you, or else be absent, I may hear of your affairs, that ye stand fast in one spirit, with one mind striving together for the faith of the Gospel." It seems that one's manner of life and the Gospel are very vitally related. The faith we have in God and His power to save and to keep us saved is revealed in a simple demonstration of our faith. We are to walk worthy of the Gospel. We are to be examples among the believers "in word, in conversation, in charity, in spirit, in faith, and in purity." 1 Timothy 4:12 One's faith in the Gospel is to be revealed and demonstrated in "conversation that becometh the Gospel of Christ." Many people are concerned about appearance and outward beauty. We should give more attention to the inner man who needs to be renewed day by day. It is not very becoming to people who are expensively and attractively dressed to live defiled and degrading lives. There is such a thing as talking in such a manner that others will be blessed and helped. There is no excuse for cheap and vulgar talk. We are judged by the things about which we talk and by the way we talk. When we were saved "we were brought forth to walk in newness of life with Him". Billy Sunday, a famous evangelist of another day, used to say, "When I was converted I lost most of my vocabulary." We as Christians are to "strive together for the faith of the Gospel". This is altogether different from striving against each other. It is true that "The strength of the pack is the dog, and the strength of the dog is the pack." Again, "in unity there is strength". So often we as Christians sing,

"Like a mighty army moves the church of God,
Brothers, we are treading where the saints have trod;
We are not divided; all one body we,
One in hope and doctrine, one in charity.
Onward Christian soldiers, marching as to war,
With the cross of Jesus going on before."

FAITH MEETS THE TEST

There are many experiences in life that test our faith. In the hour of crisis our faith is tested. Many people confuse testing and tempting. Satan tempts us with a view to getting us to yield to temptation. God does not tempt us with a view to getting us to sin. He allows us to be tested to show that we have a power and a strength to overcome. Christianity was born in a crisis and is therefore a religion for the crisis hour. So much that is called faith is a poor substitute for faith.

158

Presumption is not faith. Neither is credulity. James makes a great statement, "My brethren, count it all joy when you fall into divers temptations, knowing this that the trying of your faith worketh patience." James 1:2-3

Abraham was tested when called out of Ur of the Chaldees. He was sorely tested when he was asked to offer his only son as a sacrifice to God. This he was willing to do, knowing that God was able to raise his son up. This is in symbol and type a picture of God offering His only son and raising Him up. "And Abraham believed God and it was counted to him for righteousness." James 2:23

Job was tested and tried. He met the severest test in life. He lost his children in a disaster. He lost his property, his health, and most of his friends. Yet, in all of the testings through which Job passed, he never lost hope nor faith in God. He could say, "Though he slay me, yet will I trust him". And he could say in a virile and vibrant faith, "I know that my redeemer liveth, and that he will stand for me in the latter day." Such faith cannot be defeated. Kipling makes a striking statement in "The White Man's Burden" when he says, "Nothing is worth the making unless it makes the man".

Noah walked and worked by faith. He took God at His word. He obeyed God in a program and a project which seemed foolish. For 120 years he worked on the ark, preparing it for the saving of those who would come within it in the time of flood. "By faith Noah, being warned of God of things not seen as yet, moved with fear, prepared an ark to the saving of his house; by which he condemned the world, and became heir of the righteousness which is by faith." Hebrews 11:7

Many more examples both in the Old and the New Testament could be sighted to illustrate what we are talking about. There are today many conditions and circumstances under which our faith is tested. A real test of faith comes when a person goes from poverty to riches. Often the reverse is true, for when one goes from riches to poverty, as some do, faith is really tested. It is then that one will find out if his faith is misplaced or if he is trusting in his money, stocks, or bonds, rather than trusting in God. Many are tested and tried in some reverse, such as personal sickness, sickness of a companion, or a child. Tests come when one passes from political and social fame to obscurity. They come when one's friends forsake him or when his loved ones are taken from him.

FAITH WILL BRING VICTORY

Every child of God should desire to be a victor, and this is made possible. The apostle Paul recognized the fact that he could be victorious in Christ. He could do all things through Christ. His grace was assured. "Thanks be unto God, who giveth us the victory through our Lord Jesus Christ." 1 Corinthians 15:57 Every born-again Christian can be assured of victory over sin, Satan, and temptation in this life and in death. John, the beloved disciple, lived the life of a victor. In 1 John 5:4 we find this great truth, "For whatsoever is born of God overcometh the world: and this is the victory that overcometh the world, even our faith." No person can ever hope to be a victor unless and until after he has been "born again". We cannot be "born again" without exercising faith in Jesus Christ. Dwight L. Moody said that he was 20 years of age before he ever heard a sermon on Regeneration or the new birth. He was told to be good. This does not go far enough. No person by his good works can ever be good enough to be a Christian. John asks, "Who is he that overcometh the world, but he that believeth that Jesus is the Son of God?" 1 John 5:5 The people prepared and moved together against the wall of Jericho and the walls came tumbling down. Gideon prepared his handful of men, three

160

hundred, for victory over the enemy. They went forth with faith in God to victory. "Every man stood round about the camp in his place." Judges 7:21

All through the New Testament faith is stressed as an essential in life. It is necessary if one is to be saved. We must have faith to walk with God. We must have faith to do the work of God. We must have faith to obey the commands of Christ. Time and time again we are assured of victory if we have faith. In Revelation 21:7 "He that overcometh shall inherit all things: and I will be his God, and he shall be my son." In Revelation 12:11 the way to victory is stated: "And they overcame him by the blood of the Lamb, and by the word of their testimony; and they loved not their lives unto the death." We sing —

> "To him that overcometh God giveth a crown,
> Through faith we shall conquer, though often cast down,
> He who is our Savior, our strength will renew,
> Look ever to Jesus, he will carry you through."

CHAPTER TWENTY

THE KIND OF PERSONS WE OUGHT TO BE

"Seeing then that all these things shall be dissolved, what manner of persons ought ye to be in all holy conversation and godliness, Looking for and hasting unto the coming of the day of God, wherein the heavens being on fire shall be dissolved, and the elements shall melt with fervent heat?" 2 Peter 3:11-12 Look at the New English translation: "Since the whole universe is to break up in this way, think what devout and dedicated lives we should live."

The background for the setting of this Scripture is most interesting. Attention is directed to the fact of Christ's coming again. Not only does Peter point up this fact, but so do other writers as well. We should ask ourselves, "Since Jesus is coming back again, what kind of person should I be day by day?"

There is the Great and Final Judgment Day. This will be an appointment that all must meet, prepared or unprepared. It seems that in Peter's writing some great cataclysmic event will accompany it. A noted scientist said in my hearing, "It could be that Peter refers to what will be some great nuclear power that will cause things to melt with fervent heat and all mankind would be affected by it — and millions would be burned up." Man now has that kind of power at his disposal.

163

Peter reminds us in this same passage "That the heavens will pass away with a great noise, and the elements shall melt with fervent heat; the earth also and the works that are therein shall be burned up." In the light of Jesus' coming again and the coming of the final judgment we need to be ready at any and at all times. God has a time in mind when He will say — "It is now closing time". History will be consumated and time shall be no more.

Another fact to keep in mind is that death is always near. It was David who said, "There is but a step between me and death." The writer of Hebrews says very definitely and pointedly, "It is appointed unto man once to die and after this the judgment." No person can rationalize death out of the whole of life's experiences. God's judgment came in the days of Noah. His judgment came upon the people of Sodom and Gomorrah, even though they did not expect it.

Since all these things will come to pass what manner of persons ought we to be?

WE SHOULD BE REDEEMED PERSONS

In other words we should know that we have been "born from above". We should be sure that we have been saved, that we are the "heirs of God and joint-heirs with Jesus Christ". According to the teaching of the Bible not all who profess to be saved have been saved. Jesus asked, "Why do you call me Lord, Lord, and do not the things that I say?" And again, "Not everyone that sayeth unto me Lord, Lord shall enter into the Kingdom of Heaven, but he that doeth the will of my Father who is in heaven." Jesus said, "Many will say unto me in that day, Lord, Lord, have we not prophesied in thy name? and in thy name have cast out devils? and in thy name done many wonderful works? And then will I profess unto them, I never knew you: depart from me, ye that work iniquity." Matthew 7:22-23 Not all

164

professed Christians are the right kind of persons. Too often some of the worst of sins are committed by those who profess to belong to Christ. We conform to the world when we are enjoined to be transformed. We are called to come out from the world and live separated lives. We are to be in the world, but have no place for the world within our hearts and lives. The early Christians were known for their poverty and power, while many of us are known by our wealth and weakness. Some years ago a group of young communists were marching in Moscow chanting, "We may be hungry, we may be cold, but we change the world." General Omar Bradley said, "The most completely dedicated person I have ever met was a convinced communist." I would have to say, "The most completely dedicated person I have ever known is a committed Christian."

WE SHOULD BE MEN AND WOMEN OF PRAYER

Prayer is natural and necessary. It is just as natural for a Christian to pray as it is for one to eat. Jesus said in John 14:13-15 "And whatsoever ye shall ask in my name, that will I do, that the Father may be glorified in the Son. If ye shall ask anything in my name, I will do it. If ye love me keep my commandments." Often we have not because we ask not. Then, we ask selfishly and with a desire to consume it upon our lusts. The wrong motive moves many to pray. We are given strength when we pray. We can have Divine Wisdom when we pray. There has been much talk about prayer and Bible reading in public schools. What we need is for parents to make a place for Bible reading and prayer in the home. In prayer we are to wait upon power from on high which has been assured. The story is told of George Adam Clark climbing a dangerous Alpine peak. As he stood at the top he was suddenly pulled to his knees by his guide who said, "On

165

your knees sir! On your knees! You are not safe here except on your knees."

WE ARE TO BE A BELIEVING AND A TRUSTING PEOPLE

Some people think that it does not matter what one believes. It is of tremendous value for one to believe the right thing. A group of young people were joy riding. They stopped and asked a farmer: "Where does this road lead?" He replied, "Where do you want to go?" They replied, "Oh it does not make any difference." Then said the farmer, "If it does not make any difference where you are going, it does not make any difference which road you take."

Sound doctrine makes for sound living. "Take heed unto thyself and unto the doctrine . . . for in doing this thou shalt both save thyself, and them that hear you." 1 Timothy 4:16 We need to examine our doctrines or beliefs. We need to know what the truth is and seek to live by it. It is the truth of God that will set men free. It will also hold us to the straight and the narrow road over which we are to travel. Too many people are like the man who was talking with a friend about astrology. He said, "I didn't know that you believed in astrology." He replied, "I believe in everything a little bit." A man thought he was bragging on his preacher for being broad minded when he said, "Our preacher never preaches doctrine, nor anything else much."

WE SHOULD BE CONSISTENT CHRISTIANS

We need to take a good look at our profession. It would be good to see if we really possess that which we profess to believe. Our talk, walk, and conduct should harmonize with our profession. We are to "adorn the Gospel". In our dress, walk, and talk we are to behave as becometh the children of God. People took knowledge of Peter and John that they had

166

been with Jesus. John the beloved says, "If we say that we have fellowship with Him, and walk in darkness, we lie, and do not the truth: But if we walk in the light as he is in the light, we have fellowship one with another, and the blood of Jesus Christ His son cleanseth us from all sin." 1 John 1:6-7 A cynic once said, "A Christian is one who feels penitent on Sunday for what he did on Saturday and for what he is going to do on Monday." It could be that some of us are like the little girl who said, "Conscience is something that hurts me when my brother Tom does wrong."

WE OUGHT TO BE HAPPY PEOPLE

We can have peace, joy, and happiness within. We need to read the Beatitudes over and over again in Matthew chapters 5, 6, and 7. Note the situations under which we are to be happy. Jesus said, "In the world ye shall have tribulation, but be of good cheer for I have overcome the world." He also said, "My peace I give unto you, my peace I leave with you . . ." Paul in a prison could rejoice that he was counted worthy to suffer for Christ's sake. We can sing, "I have the joy, joy, joy, joy down in my heart, down in my heart to stay." Redeemed people should be the happiest people in the world. It seems that Psalm 1 is a vivid picture of a man of God who is blessed and happy. It seems to me that no person lost in sin could be very happy in the light of the fact that Jesus is coming again, that the Judgment will come to all, and that no person can escape the inevitable appointment with death.

WE OUGHT TO BE SPIRIT FILLED
PEOPLE

The Spirit is promised to those who wait upon His coming. The early Christians waited in Jerusalem for his presence and power. They were all together in one place

167

praying when he came upon them. In Ephesians 5:18 are these words, "And be not drunk with wine, wherein is excess; but be filled with the Spirit." On the day of Pentecost the Christians were all filled with the Holy Spirit. There is a picture of Gideon in the Old Testament where the Spirit of God clothed himself with Gideon.

WE ARE TO BE AN EXPECTANT
PEOPLE

We should attempt great things for God. At the same time we should expect great things from God. We see occasions where Jesus could do no more mighty works in some places because of a lack of faith or the little faith of the people. He said, "Be it done unto you according to your faith." And again he said, "O ye of little faith." Then again we read, "And he could do no mighty works there because of their lack of faith." When Carey launched the mighty Missionary Movement he stressed two facts – namely "Attempt great things for God and expect great things from God." A young man was reading 1 Corinthians 15 to John Newton who was almost blind. Newton stopped him at verse 10 and said, "By the grace of God I am what I am." Then he added, "I am not what I ought to be, not what I hope to be, but thank God, what I am, I am by the grace of God." Unless we attempt great things for God we will not expect very much to happen.

WE OUGHT TO BE CHEERFUL AND
GENEROUS GIVERS

We should give of our substance cheerfully and gladly. This is most inclusive. We are to honor God with all of our substance. This means life, service, and material substance. We are to give good measure, "pressed down and shaken together, and running over". We are to give "according to the blessing of the Lord thy God which he hath given" to us. We are taught that the liberal soul shall grow fat. We are also taught that the Lord loves the cheerful giver. Each is to give "according to the blessing of the Lord thy God". We are to give as we purpose in our hearts. God always uses a bigger shovel than we do. This is why we can keep on giving. We are to keep on giving as long as God keeps giving to us. The stingy and the greedy person cannot be much Christian. Jesus warns, "Beware of covetousness: for a man's life consisteth not in the abundance of the things which he possesseth." Luke 12:15 God is expecting much more from some of us than He expects from others. Read Luke 12:48 "For unto whomsoever much is given, of him shall much be required: and to whom men have committed much, of him they will ask the more."

WE ARE TO WITNESS TO OTHERS

In other words we are under obligation to God to tell others about the good news that came to us when Jesus found us and saved us. Every saved person has a story to tell to others. Jesus came to seek and to save that which was lost. Paul, after he met Jesus on the Damascus road, felt indebted to a lost world. Not only did he care for and have concern for the Jews but for the Gentiles as well. We, as witnesses, are to tell others. Jesus was moved with compassion as He looked upon the multitude that was scattered as sheep without a shepherd. The Bible says, "He that winneth souls is wise" and "they that be wise shall shine as the brightness of the firmament and they that turn many to righteousness as the stars for ever and ever." In Luke 16 we see a picture of a rich man dying and after death he had more concern for his five lost brothers than he had while he was on this earth. Could it be that many of us will wake up in Hell longing to warn those we love, lest they come to that place of torment? When Jesus

169

saved and healed the Gadarene Demoniac he told him to go and show himself to his kindred and friends. It seems that this would have been sufficient proof of the power of Jesus to save. This is indeed a day of "good tidings" and we should not hold our peace. Andrew found his brother and told him about Jesus. He told him that he had found the Messiah and that he should come and see for himself. Philip was brought to the Ethiopian and led him to faith in Jesus Christ. The man who was born blind knew that Jesus had healed him. He wanted to tell others even though he did not understand the miracle that had taken place. When the woman of Samaria met Jesus and was saved she went into the village and told the men of that place what had happened. She invited them to come and see Jesus. This is something that a Junior boy or girl can do. This is something that any adult can do if he has met the Savior and trusted Him. Surely, every one of us should be about our Father's business while we have time and opportunity.

Look at the text again: "Seeing then that all these things shall be dissolved, what manner of persons ought we to be in all holy conversation and godliness."

About the Author

J. Guy Cothran was born in lower Greenville County May 24, 1897. He was educated in the public schools of the county. He graduated with an A. B. degree from Furman University in 1922. He was graduated from the Southern Baptist Theological Seminary with a Th.M. degree in 1925.

He was licensed to preach by the Cedar Shoals Baptist Church in 1920. In 1924 he was called to be pastor of the Baptist Church in English, Kentucky and was ordained by the Walnut Street Baptist Church, Louisville, Kentucky.

Cothran served in the Naval Reserve Force and took training at the University of Georgia. He has taught in high school, serving as principal in three schools. In his last pastorate at Beaverdam he taught for four years at Anderson College.

Cothran has served these Baptist churches: Emannuel Baptist Church, Panama City, Florida; First Church, Benton, Arkansas; First Church, Princeton, Kentucky; and First Church, Arkadelphia, Arkansas. He also served for 3 years and 3 months as director of a $1,500,000 campaign for the Baptist schools of Kentucky. He has served on committees and boards statewide and Southwide. He has been busy since retirement writing, serving as interim pastor, conducting revivals, and serving as supply. He has traveled rather extensively.